Higher RMPS
at Stewart's Melville College

ISBN: 9798379290788

"Learning is the only thing the mind never exhausts, never fears, and never regrets."
-Leonardo da Vinci.

CONTENTS

1 BELIEFS ABOUT GOD

The Qur'an (the holy book of Islam) states that a believer should maintain belief in God, angels, prophets, revealed books or scriptures, and life after death. Some Muslims also believe that 'Divine decree and determining' should be included i.e. the belief that certain events have been planned by God. These six 'articles of faith' can be grouped into three main characters called the 'fundamentals of belief': belief in Divine Unity, belief in prophethood, and belief in resurrection and the hereafter.

Divine Unity

The central message of the Qur'an is the oneness of God, rather than just His existence. Whilst it is not the only monotheistic religion, it is important to explore what Muslims specifically believe about God.

The Arabic word for God is *Allah* and this can be used interchangeably with the word God. The Qur'an describes God's attributes and character so that humans can have a deeper understanding of God and fulfil their role as Allah's representative on earth.

Within Islam, the most key belief is that God is Tawhid; this means one-ness or unity. God is the absolute or the alone - nothing rivals Him and nothing is like Him. The Oneness of God can be understood when one looks at any single manifestation of Divine design or complexity, which points to a single source and purpose.

Surah 2:225 says "there is no deity except Him, the Ever-Living, the Sustainer of [all] existence..."

The concept of tawhid also emphasizes the idea that God is the only one worthy of worship, and all other deities or objects of worship are false. When a person tries to like God to any created thing, or to suggest that other things in the universe somehow share in God's creative power, or have His knowledge or ability to guide or forgive – this is known as the sin of **shirk**.

Islam considers the sin of shirk, or associating partners with God, to be the greatest sin deserving of punishment. Shirk involves attributing power or perfection to created beings or abstract forces other than God. In pre-Qur'anic societies, shirk was expressed through the worship of idols, statues, or effigies representing gods and goddesses, which were venerated alongside or in place of God.

Modern theologians argue that idolatry is no longer practiced in the form of physical veneration, but rather in a metaphorical sense. The idols of today's world such as money, power, and celebrity are just as dangerous to the human soul as the idols of the past. The Qur'an warns believers that even they are not immune to shirk, which can mean worshipping idols alongside God, not just in place of God.

Belief in prophethood

Muslims believe that God communicates with humanity through revelation, and He has sent prophets and messengers to guide humanity throughout history. The Qur'an (the Muslim holy book) is believed to be the literal word of God and therefore is a useful source of knowledge when it comes to understanding more about Allah.

Although the popular Muslim tradition states that God has 99 names, the Qur'an suggests that God has innumerable names and attributes of perfection. God is described as omniscient, omnipotent, omnipresent, and immanent but yet transcendent. He is the Creator of all things and stands above all matter and materiality. When Muslims talk of God being 'eternal' or 'infinite', they are admitting that He is beyond human knowledge and reasoning. However, at the same time as believing that Allah is beyond all things, they also believe that God is immanent, which means that He is closer to each human than their heartbeat and knows even our unspoken thoughts, fears and hopes.

> *'It was We who created man, and We know even the secret suggestions of his soul makes to him; for We are nearer to him that [his] jugular vein.'*
>
> *Surah 50:1*

Within the Qur'an Allah has many different descriptions – in fact, it teaches that Allah has 99 names. Each of these 99 names relates to a particular attribute of Allah, which in theory makes Him easier to understand and relate to.

The Qur'an states that everything in the universe is structured and ordered according to a predetermined plan from God. This plan determines the nature, duration, and effect of each person's existence in time and space.

The Muslim belief in predestination is puzzling when their belief in free will is also considered. If Allah has a plan which uses the evil that people do, then is Allah to blame for the evil people do? How can free will fit in with Allah's master plan? If what we do suits Allah's purposes how can He punish us in Hell?

Muslims believe that Allah does not force us to do anything. We do have the power to make choices. However, Allah is so infinite in His power that He knows what each individual will do before He does it. Knowing something will happen is not the same thing as causing that thing to happen. The consequences of each choice or decision are used by Allah to test people. Divine punishment serves a purpose in bringing people back to God, it is an opportunity to learn and ultimately gain a place in heaven.

Belief in resurrection and the hereafter

Muslims believe that there will be a final judgement day in which Allah will judge them upon their actions in this life. It is here that they will be rewarded or punished according to how they have lived their lives on earth, and how well they have submitted to God's commands. This will be explored in a later chapter - Akhira - but it should be very clear that Allah is very much the focus of life within Islam.

The impact of beliefs about God

It should be noted that Islam translates to submission (or surrender) and that a Muslim is 'one who submits'. It is said that developing awareness of Allah is like opening your eyes for the first time as a baby. Once you are awake to that reality then all of life will be different from that point.

This awareness is known as 'Taqwa' which is also sometimes translated as 'fear'. But this is not fear of punishment but rather a worry that an individual isn't doing enough or living in a way that's honoring Allah. As it's believed that everything comes from Him, there is obviously a deep sense of gratitude towards Him for giving this life.

To many, Allah's immanence proves that He is actively involved in His creation as He is close with every human today. It could be viewed as comforting as they can trust that Allah will always be with them, supporting them in any times of trial. There's no doubt that Islamophobia remains rife throughout the world, and the belief in Allah's immanence provides a source of comfort in these situations as they would feel as if they were not alone as Allah is there.

But it could also be seen that because it's believed that Allah is always with us – seeing everything – this means that Muslims may feel like their life is always under a microscope as Allah even knows what you're thinking.

This means that a Muslim would trust that Allah always understands their Niyah (intention) though and so will understand if actions go awry due to unforeseen consequences and would not judge them so harshly. After all, if you stick to the rules there's really nothing to fear!

It's worth bearing in mind that Muslims believe that Allah's judgement can result in direct consequences. For example, the Qur'an recounts the story of Adam and Hawah (who readers might know better as Eve) who disobeyed God by eating from the tree of knowledge - he cast them out of the garden.

This could perhaps result in Muslims feeling anxious knowing that there can be severe consequences for wrongdoing. But equally it can be viewed as a positive as this means that there would be no need to take direct revenge upon enemies - knowing that Allah will have seen their wrongdoing and will be Just in His approach.

As mentioned before, Islam wouldn't even exist without God given that everything comes from Him to begin with. Although there are other beliefs in Islam, they would be pointless without belief in God. Given that God is the ultimate judge and that this effects a Muslims' life for eternity, it is natural that this life must be focused on pleasing Him. Awareness of Allah alters every moment of life.

An example of this would be God's power. Muslims believe that He can truly change their lives so they know they must live their whole lives as an act of worship to Him - this clearly impacts even their daily lives. These beliefs ensure that Muslims maintain a humble life and care for others because they know everything they have is only because of Allah.

Lastly, they are the most significant of all Muslim beliefs because they can live a life safe in the knowledge that God is all-loving, and all-forgiving and therefore they can always maintain a positive attitude and find happiness.

- Free will
- suffering
- Khalifa

2 NATURE OF HUMAN BEINGS

Muslims believe that humans were originally created by Allah as the 'pinnacle of creation'. Humanity was gifted with attributes that no other creature has, i.e., free will. Muslims believe that although Angels existed before humans, we were made to have knowledge that they did not have i.e. free will - and so are superior to them. As the Qur'an describes, they were ordered to bow down to Adam.

Muslims believe that it is important to recognise that we all have a 'ruh' or soul that will last forever, whereas our bodies – made from the earth – are empty vessels without this. The Quran describes the human as actually having been created from clay, the material part, but it also talks about God teaching mankind his intellect, and about having the spirit of

God within him and that God breathed into mankind of His spirit.

But the Quran also states clearly that God has "shown him the two highways" - truth and falsehood. Ultimately, Muslims believe that life is a test, in which Allah sees every aspect of life and will judge each individual on the basis of what He sees.

Free Will

Free will is the ability to make our own decisions. Each individual has the freedom to choose between good and evil - between submitting to Allah or not.

Whilst humans are free to do as they want, they have also been given an in-built sense of right and wrong. This is called the 'fitrah' - human beings' natural moral compass. Instinctively we know that hurting others is bad and to seek out kindness, empathy, and love.

This 'moral law within' is shown by the conscience. But of course, we are free to listen to that conscience - ensuring that it's sensitive and well training - or we can crush it and ignore it. We can choose to train our conscience through prayer, study of the Qu'ran, attendance at the Mosque, in following the Hadith or equally, we can choose not to. In other words, we can use or misuse the gift of free will.

As Allah is all loving (Al Wadud) it would be illogical to think that He would not provide a guide for humans on how to use their freewill. Muslims believe this guidance comes from the Qu'ran, but as it says in *Qu'ran 2:256 ' There shall be no compulsion in [acceptance of] the religion'.* Allah isn't forcing people to choose but simply showing them the choice.

Human life is viewed as a trial or test - this is individual - so each person will face different experiences. Some of these experiences will arise as a result of misusing free will, and the consequences of those actions may impact that person or the people around them.

In practice, we make choices together, whether that's as a family unit or within a particular society or culture. Many of our personal decisions may well be shaped and patterned by our upbringing, our peer group, or our society. But at the end of the day, we are still free to conform or to rebel.

It's important to note that whilst Muslims believe that each of us control our own destinies, they also believe that everything in life has been planned for by God.

Shi'a Muslims believe that God *knows* what will happen, but this doesn't mean that He *decides* it. They believe that God can see everything that happens - past, present, and future. God knows what choices people will make, but they still have the free will to make these choices for themselves.

Qu'ran 13:11 God does not change the conditions of a people for the worse unless they change what is in themselves.

Suffering

Suffering is the bearing or undergoing of pain or distress. Within Islam, it is possible to view suffering as a result of evil.

There are two types of evil:

- moral evil - the acts of humans which are considered to be morally wrong

Evil is a cause of suffering

- natural evil - natural disasters, such as earthquakes or **tsunamis**

These two types of evil can work together in that human evil can make natural evil worse. For example, whilst a drought brought on by lack of rainfall causes crops to fail (natural evil), the policies of a government can make the food shortages for the poorest people worse (moral evil).

There are a number of explanations for evil within Islamic belief:

The Qur'an teaches that evil originates from the refusal of Shaytan, also called Iblis, to bow down to Adam when ordered to by Allah. For his disobedience Iblis was cast out of Heaven by Allah, and he vowed that in revenge he would spend eternity trying to tempt humans to do evil.

In the Last Sermon (or Farewell Speech), the Prophet Muhammad warned Muslims about Shaytan by saying *'Beware of Shaytan, he is desperate to divert you from the worship of Allah.'*

However, it's important to note that Shaytan isn't the cause of suffering he is only tempting humans to misuse their free will. Muslims must choose between right, using the guidance of Allah, and wrong, following the temptations of the Devil.

Many Muslims believe that suffering can be caused by the selfishness and evil of human beings which leads to bad decisions. They can overcome suffering in their own lives and help to ease the suffering of others by following Allah's path. This path is set out in the Qur'an and in the Sunnah.

Since they believe that Allah is in overall control, Muslims often try to see a purpose in suffering. They sometimes understand it as Allah's way of educating them, or as retribution for a wrong they have committed, or as a test. If they respond with patience and remain firm in their faith, they will have increased reward in the afterlife. For some Muslims, the test of suffering is perceived as a blessing.

Living in this world with its numerous distractions, sometimes God causes us to suffer to remind us of Him, so that we remember in the midst of all of our activities what truly is important and why we are here on this earth. In the Hadith, Muhammad is recorded as saying:

'When God desires the redemption of His people, He causes them to suffer in this world. But when He is averse, He leaves them to transgress until death overtakes.'

Another universal point that has been the focused on by Muslim philosophers is that opposites produce opposites. Existence and non-existence, life and death, permanence and non-permanence, youth and old-age are linked with each other. As the 21st century Persian poet, Sa'di said:

"Treasure and snake and flower and thorn and sorrow and happiness come together."

How do Muslims respond to evil and suffering?

- Have **sabr** (patience) and endure – after all, life is a test.

Sabr is one of the two parts of faith (the other being *shukr*-thankfulness/gratitude) in Islam. It teaches people to remain spiritually steadfast when facing opposition or encountering problems, setbacks, or unexpected and unwanted results. It is patience in the face of all unexpected and unwanted outcomes.

- Repentance

In the Qur'an Allah says that he will forgive anyone who sincerely repents, just as he forgave Adam and Eve when they were tempted by Shaytan and ate the forbidden fruit. They offered 'du'a' or voluntary prayer for what they had done:

Qu'ran 7:23: Our Lord, we have wronged ourselves, and if You do not forgive us and have mercy upon us, we will surely be among the losers.

- Act in the way they want to be treated

Muslims are also expected to follow Allah's example of justice, mercy and forgiveness in their treatment of other people:

Qu'ran 7:199 'Hold to forgiveness; command what is right; but turn away from the ignorant.'

Therefore, Muslims believe that when they see people who are suffering, they should treat them with mercy. When they see evil actions, they should ensure that justice is done.

Khalifas - Caretakers of the Earth

For many Muslims, the guiding principles on the environment are that Allah has made everything and has entrusted creation to humans for them to look after as a sacred trust.

Human beings are stewards or guardians (khulafa' – the plural of khalifah in Arabic) and they will have to give an account of how they carried out their guardianship of the environment on the Day of Judgement. This is supported in both the Qur'an and the Hadith:

- *Qu'ran 6:165 It is He who has appointed you vicegerent on the earth..."*

- *"The world is beautiful and verdant, and verily God, the exalted, has made you His stewards in it, and He sees how you acquit yourselves" (Hadith)*

Muslims may understand and apply these principles to the question of looking after the environment in a variety of ways. Muslim leaders, representing all the major groups of Muslims, drew up a Seven Year Plan in 2009. The aim was to improve the environment. Actions include: limiting the use of new resources, encouraging recycling, and developing guidance for business on how best to protect the environment from exploitation.

Sharing Resources

Although the earth is created to serve the purposes of man, it should never be degraded in any way – contaminated or immoderately exploited. Its resources are available to humanity, but are to be used in ways that are sustainable and without harmful impact to the environment and the ecological balance. The Quran tells us,

Qur'an 25:63 'The servants of the Lord of Mercy are those who walk gently upon the earth...'

Islamic teachings oppose using resources in excess or in pursuit of an opulent lifestyle; extravagant excess by some typically deprives others of a basic standard of decent and secure living.

There should always be justice ('adl) in resource distribution. Allah SWT instructs us about the sharing of resources, using the example of the tribe of Thamud:

Qur'an 54:28 'And let them know that the water [of their wells] is to be divided between them, with each share of water equitably apportioned.'

Land Preservation

The Prophet was also a pioneer when it came to land preservation and providing sanctuary for wildlife. He designated special areas where water, wildlife, and forestry use would be restricted (haram) or left alone altogether (hima).

 The Prophet believed that animals, land, and water were not the possessions of mankind, but rather provisions from Allah to use in moderation and wisdom.

The Quran 7:31 says, *'...waste not by excess, for Allah loves not the wasters.'*

Sunni Muslims have created haram zones where people have to respect natural resources and not exploit anything that is there. They have also created animal reserves to protect wildlife and forests. These actions aim to re-establish nature as Allah wants it to be.

Recycling

Recycling should be a reflex. In many places it's as easy as placing non-food remains in the appropriate bin. And where composting is available (which can be anywhere food is grown), most waste can be reused as nutrients to fertilize the soil for further growing of fruits and vegetables. Things that we typically throw in the trash can be re-used in one way or another. Metals, plastics, and glass should not be going to landfills as they can be reused or recycled. The paper that comes from a chopped-down tree is worth far more than a single use.

Qur'an 30:41 tells us, *'Corruption has appeared on land and sea because of what the hands of humans have wrought, that He may make them taste a part of that which they have done, in order that they may return [to guidance].'*

3 BELIEFS ABOUT MUHAMMAD

Muslims believe in a loving Allah who would not allow people to go through life unaware of how they should be living.

Muslims believe that humankind craves understanding of life and the universe. Humankind looks for a closer relationship with Allah but at the same time his efforts are frustrated due to misconceptions and distractions. He strays from the right path to a closer relationship with Allah.

Muslims believe that Allah provided for humanity all that they need for a happy life: whether for their physical or emotional needs; or for their knowledge of the nature of the universe; or for guidance on morality.

For Muslims, the greatness and power of Allah means that He

cannot communicate directly with humans, and yet His compassion means that He cannot just leave them to make a mess of their lives. The channel of communication between Allah and humanity is known as 'Risalah'. Muslims believe that Allah passes His message directly into the minds of prophets (Rasul) who pass this directly to the rest of humanity.

Qur'an 42:13 'Allah chooses for Himself whoever He pleases, and guides to Himself those who turn [to Him].'

These messages are known as revelations. Muslims believe that Allah has communicated to people through many prophets including Adam, Abraham and Jesus. The prophets of Judaism and Christianity are also the prophets of Islam. The five major prophets before Muhammad were Adam, Nuh (Noah), Ibrahim (Abraham), Musa (Moses) and Isa (Jesus). However, the prophet which Muslims consider to be most valuable is Muhammad. This is the first revelation Muhammad received from Allah.

The Seal

The prophet Muhammad holds a very special place for Muslims because he was the last of the long succession of prophets to whom specific revelations were made. He was the final seal of all who had gone before. In the eyes of Muslims, the prophet Muhammad is the perfect example of how to live in a way that is pleasing to God. He is a means by which they can achieve their goal of living their life in submission to God.

Muhammad's Early Life

Muhammad was born in Makkah (or Mecca) in 570CE. Although he was born into the ruling tribe – the Quraysh - he suffered some hardship as a child since both his parents died and he was cared for by his grandfather and later by his uncle.

17

As a young man Muhammad worked as a shepherd. He was hard-working and trustworthy. At this time Muhammad became known as al-Amin, the trustworthy one. His hard work and fair dealings helped him catch the attention of a wealthy widow called Kadijah, and they married.

At that time life in Makkah was corrupt. There was much fighting and gambling. It was common to worship false gods (idols). There was also a lack of compassion for the poor, old and sick. Muhammad spent time alone thinking about these problems and meditating in caves in the mountains outside Makkah.

The Night of Power

In 610CE, in a cave on Mount Hira, above Mecca, Muhammad had an experience that would be the defining moment of his life. According to sources, Jibril seized him and squeezed the Prophet to the point that he thought he was going to die, and issued a command. He said, "Iqraa' (Read!)." The Prophet Muhammad was illiterate and responded that he could not read. Two more times, Jibril repeated the command and the Prophet responded with the same answer. Then, Jibril revealed the first verses of the Qur'an to the Prophet:

Qur'an 96:1-5 'Read in the name of your Lord who created - created man from a clot. Read: for your Lord is Most Bountiful, who teaches by the pen, teaches man that which he knew not.'

After this encounter, the Prophet ran from the cave. Muslim sources say that the experience was so overwhelming that whenever he would look back behind him, he would see Jibril completely covering the horizon. The person that the Prophet ran to for comfort was his wife, Khadijah. When he reached home, he told her repeatedly to cover him. He then told her what had happened in the cave. She replied by saying that his vision was true and that she did not believe that with his character Allah would humiliate him:

Never! By Allah, Allah will never disgrace you. You keep good relations with your relatives, help the poor, serve your guests generously, and assist those hit with calamities. (Hadith)

Khadijah then took the Prophet to her cousin Waraqah, a biblical scholar. After hearing the account, he told Muhammad that he had the signs of prophecy. Muhammad had joined the long line of prophets sent by Allah to call society to monotheism and to leading righteous lives.

Muslim tradition is unclear how long it was before Muhammad received his next revelation. Some sources say six months, others as much as two years. However long it was, Muhammad was left in a time of doubt and frustration. Eventually, the revelations did begin again and continued until his death in 632CE.

Muhammad relayed these messages through speech, but people quickly realised that the message was liable to be lost if it was not recorded. So, from a very early date, people began copying it down.

It's important to note that Muhammad was not the author of the Qur'an but rather the words were *revealed* to him. Therefore, to Muslims, the Qur'an is the infallible word of God.

The establishment of Islam

Muhammad's role in Islam became clear – he must deliver the message of Allah, which was a monotheistic message. This was contrary to the established culture which was centred around belief of many gods and the worship of idols. It was deeply unsettling for them to hear this new message, and whilst at first it could be disregarded, as Muhammad attracted more followers – it soon became a real threat.

The tension grew to such an extent that a tribal war would be inevitable. In 619CE Muhammad's beloved wife Khadijah died and shortly after that, his uncle died too. At this point, Muhmmad lost the protection of his tribe and was in real danger. A plot to assassinate him was uncovered and many of his followers were experiencing severe persecution.

The Night Journey

It was at this time that Muhammad experienced what was arguably one of the most intense spiritual experiences of his life. According to Islamic tradition, Muhammad's night journey, also known as *Isra* and *Mi'raj,* occurred in the year 621CE. It is believed that the journey took place on a winged creature known as Buraq, and began in Mecca where Muhammad was resting in the Kaaba.

The journey began with the arrival of the angel Gabriel, who brought Buraq to Muhammad. Muhammad mounted the created and began his journey to Jerusalem, where he arrived at the Al-Aqsa Mosque, which was then the furthest mosque.

Qur'an 17:1 Glory to God, he did take His servant for a journey by night from the sacred mosque to the furthest mosque, whose precincts We did bless in order that We might show him some of Our signs: for He is the One who heareth, and seeth (all things).

At the mosque, Muhammad led a prayer with all the prophets who had preceded him, including Abraham, Moses, and Jesus. After the prayers, Gabriel took Muhammad to Haven, where he met with Allah and received the commandment for Muslims to pray five times a day.

The journey is considered a significant event in Islamic history, as it is believed that it demonstrated Muhammad's prophethood and strengthened the faith of his followers.

The Migration

Deprived of the political protection of his uncle – Abu Talib – it was clear that his days in Mecca were numbered. However, help appeared from an unexpected source.

In the town of Yathrib, later called Medina (the city of the Prophet), around 250 miles from Mecca, tribal rivalries had become deadly, and the people desperately needed a peacemaker. They had heard that Muhammed was a trustworthy man, said they invited him to solve their disputes.

Slowly, and almost unnoticed at first, the Muslims of Mecca began to leave. It was only when Muhammad and his closest companions were left, that the Quraysh realised what was happening. Mindful that this migration could lead to the growth of Islam, the elders set out in a plan to kill Muhammad.

According to tradition, Muhammad learned of the plot to assassinate him and he drew up plans to flee. On the night of the planned assassination, he left his young cousin Ali sleeping in his bed. The would-be assassins approached the bedchamber only to discover the boy sleeping soundly. Muhammad and his companion Abu Bakr were able to escape on camelback.

Stories describe how Muhammad and Abu Bakr took shelter in a cave, and how their pursuers would have found them, had they not been fooled by a spider's web that had been woven miraculously across the mouth of the cave - giving the impression that no one could have entered. The following day, Muhammad and his companion continued onto Yathrib. Where they received a warm welcome - from the migrants of Mecca and the people of Yathrib who had given them refuge.

The establishment of Medina

Muhammad's goal among the people of Yathrib was much the same as his larger mission - to bring a message of unity and peace. As his work succeeded, the town became known as the 'city of the Prophet' - Medina.

To the divided tribes of Medina, Muhammad offered the idea of unity, but even as he spread the word of Islam, he did not challenge the beliefs of other faiths. Islam had its roots in Judaism and Christianity and treated their believers as people of the book. God had revealed himself and his word many times before, to prophet like Abraham, Moses, and Jesus, but each time people went astray.

It was in his second year in Medina that Muhammad built the first mosque – which became the model for later Islamic architecture. Whilst the mosque was the home of Muhammad and his family, it opened onto an enclosed courtyard where people gather to hear him.

In 624CE Muhammad declared that prayer should be directed toward Mecca rather than Jerusalem. Against the wall facing Mecca, the *qibla* wall, he built a roofed shelter supported by pillars made of palm trunks from which he could lead prayer. In 628CE a *minbar*, or pulpit, was added so that Muhammad was raised above the crowd in order to be more visible. It was from here that he also declared new laws and settled disputes. The mosque was not just for worship but combined political, judicial, and religious functions.

Muhammad's marriages

Muhammad's first marriage to Khadijah, lasted almost 25 years and was monogamous throughout. But following her death in 619CE he married Sawda, an early convert to Islam and the widow of one of his close followers. Following the migration to Medina, it is thought that he then married a further nine times, mostly to widows but he also made at least two political marriages: the first to Maria, a slave girl; the second to a Jewess capture in battle.

By far the most controversial of Muhammad's marriages was to Aisha, the daughter of his close friend Abu Bakr. Their marriage was arranged when she was around ten years old: sources do not specify when she went to live him but whilst this undoubtedly would be seen as abusive in today's world, it was a common occurrence amongst the Bedouin tribes. It was not unheard of in Muhammad's time for boys and girls to be promised to each other in marriage almost as soon as they were born – particularly if it was politically advantageous. Such marriages were not consummated until both parties had entered adulthood. In seventh century Arabia that would be the early teen years - which was wholly in keeping with the customs of the day.

Muhammad's later life: the conquest of Mecca

While Muhammad was in Medina, his opponents in Mecca were gathering forces to wipe out the Muslims. His enemies were not Jews or Christians, but the non-believers, the idolaters. For years, Muhammad had tried to bring Islam to the people of Mecca peacefully, but now it was time to fight.

The Muslims were outnumbered and faced their own tribes - brother fighting brother, son against father. They came armed with a powerful weapon, however: a passionate belief in their faith. Muhammad's troops fought with every confidence that God's will was guiding them. This struggle lasted until 630CE, when Muhammad had gathered a much stronger army and Mecca finally surrendered.

Muhammad's first act upon conquering Mecca was to announce a general amnesty for all those who had previously opposed him. Upon witnessing this mercy, a number of the Quraysh converts to

Islam, although it was clear they did not have to. Then, Muhammad smashed all of the idols that had filled the *Ka'bah*. Whilst the physical signs of idolatry were removed, it was up to the individuals to believe what they wanted. Muhammad once again reiterated that there can be no compulsion in religion, and that everyone must be free to practice their own beliefs as long as they extended the same courtesy to others.

The farewell sermon

In the tenth year of his mission, Muhammad performed a Hajj (pilgrimage) to Mecca that attracted vast crowds. He stood on the 'Mount of Mercy' on the plains to give what would be his last sermon. In it he reaffirmed basis for morality and laid out clear instructions for life including the five pillars:

"O People! Listen to me in earnest, worship Allah, say your five daily prayers, fast during month of Ramadan, and give your wealth in Zakat. Perform Hajj if you can afford it."

Muhammad died in the spring of 632CE after a higher fever. Some denied that he was gone forever, believing that he might one day return. But Abu Bakr quickly more to quash this belief saying: 'If anyone worships Muhammad, let them know that Muhammad is dead. If anyone worships God, God is the One that lives, the Everlasting.'

4 AKHIRA: DAY OF JUDGMENT; AL-JANNAH; JAHANNAM

All Muslims believe in *Akhirah*, or life after death, and that human life is divided into two sections – each individual's life on earth, and the eternal life that follows. Since our earthly lives are short in comparison with the eternal, it is obvious that eternal life is far more important. This life is simply a preparation; many Muslims would say a test, for the life to come.

People's lives in this world are necessary because they enable them to understand the concept of eternity for which they have been created. But it also serves as a training ground in which they are prepared for the eventual transition, via death, to their permanent existence in the world to come, the realm of the hereafter.

Life in the world as it is now should be viewed as just as important as the world to come, simply because one's position with regard to God in the afterlife depends very much on the nature of one's relationship with God in the here and now.

Death is treated as a matter of fact in the Qur'an as it something that comes to all human beings. As it says in Qur'an 3:185, *'every soul shall have a taste of death.'*

The Qur'an does not go into great detail about the process of death. But it does say that at the moment life ceases, the soul will be separated from the body. The body is then committed to the Earth, symbolising human beings physical return to the minerals and elements used in their initial creation.

The 'intermediate realm'

From that time, some Muslim traditions teach that the soul exists in an intermediate state called 'Barzakh' which falls between death and Judgement Day. There are many different beliefs about its nature. One such tradition affirms that the angel of death, Izrail, will question the dead about their faith. Those who fail the test will be punished immediately, whilst those who pass will be taken straight to heaven. Other Muslim traditions claim that the soul simply 'sleeps' until the Last Day so that it will only seem like a moment between death and resurrection, even if centuries have passed.

The 'End of the World'

At some point in the future, at a time unknown by anyone but Allah, the universe as we know it will cease to exist. The Qur'an paints a vivid picture of a world that will literally spin out of control as Allah 'rolls up the world like a carpet.' This time will begin with an initial trumpet blast:

Qur'an 39:68: 'The Trumpet will be sounded, when all that it are in the heavens and on earth will swoon, except such as it will please

God to exempt.'

Traditionally, it is believed that at this point all living things will die. There is then a second trumpet blast to call the dead back to life: graves will open, and the dead will rise up with their physical bodies perfectly restored. Trembling with fear, they will ask:

Qur'an 36:52. 'Ah! Woe unto us! Who has raised us up from our beds of repose?

The final Judgement

The whole of humanity will be led to the 'plain of judgement' where each person's life will be assessed. The Qur'an described that the Record (of Deeds) will be placed (open); the prophets and the witnesses will be brought forward and a just decision pronounced between them. On that day, humans will be shown the true nature and significance of everything that they ever did, said or thought.

According to Muslim tradition each of us have a Record of Deeds being written in this life right now. Each of us have two recording angels with us at all times - writing down the decisions we make as they happen. Allah does not need this in order to make a judgement because he knows everything, but rather, it can be set before each individual at the moment of judgement to be certain that His judgement is absolutely fair.

The day of judgement is said to take a thousand years, as each individual faces their own decision, but this time will pass in the 'twinkling of an eye'. Humanity will be sorted into three groups: those who are handed their book of life in their left hand are destined for hell, whereas those who received it in their right hand are destined for salvation in heaven. However, the 'foremost of the foremost' are those who are destined for union with Allah Himself, in a realm that is beyond all description and understanding.

Al Jannah (heaven)

Paradise, or Heaven, is often referred to as 'Al Jannah', the garden, with an abundance of fresh cool water, and this is a fitting symbol for luxuriant sheltered ease in a hot desert climate. All is comfortable and well-appointed in the garden, where the saved recline on soft cushions and enjoy good food and a heavenly drink that thrills and satisfies without intoxicating.

Qur'an 47:15 'Here is a Parable of the Garden which the righteous are promises; in it are rivers of water incorruptible; rivers of milk of which the taste never changes; rivers of wine, a joy to those who rive; and rivers of honey pure and clear.'

The descriptions are vivid and detailed, but most important are heaven's spiritual joys, whose appeals far surpass the more physical delights that tempt us so much in this world. It is also believed that husbands and their wives and their children will be together in heaven.

It's said that Al Jannah has eight gates through which Muslims can enter after their resurrection on Judgment Day and each has a different day that indicates the kind of righteous deed you need to have done to pass through. For example, the 'Baab Al-Hajj' gate is for those who participated in the Hajj, the annual pilgrimage to Mecca.

According to Muslim scholars, there are multiple levels to Jannah – with some saying 100, some saying limitless, and others saying 6236 – which is the number of verses in the Qur'an. In early biography of Muhammad, it's said that while he was living, Muhammad visited Allah by passing through seven levels of heaven with Jibril – finding the prophet Moses on the 6th level and Abraham above him on the 7th.

Jahannam (hell)

On the other hand, Hell, 'Jahannam', the place of fire, is a place of continuous torment. The inhabitants are chained up, given boiling water and pus to drink and garments of fire to wear. Boiling water is poured over their heads, and when their skins are too burnt to feel pain, new skins will be given to them. If they try to escape, then there are hooks of iron that drag them back in and any remorse of pleading for forgiveness is entirely in vain.

The implication of the Qur'an is clear: those who go to hell will suffer there forever. If we reflect on all of this, we will understand that many find the idea of Allah punishing evil people hard to reconcile with His mercy, but it is suggested that no one will go to Jahannam unless absolutely determined to do so:

Qur'an 92:14-16 'Therefore do I warn you of a Fire blazing fiercely; None shall reach it but those most unfortunate ones. Who give the lie to truth and turn their backs.'

5 LIVING ACCORDING TO THE FIVE PILLARS

The Five Pillars of Islam are an important and integral part of a Muslim's practice of Islam. Muslims consider the practice of these five basic duties as central to their lives as Muslims. They are the main means to a life that will lead to paradise.

Shahadah

The first pillar of Islam is the proclamation of faith. The simple confession of faith is well known: *'I bear witness that there is no god but Allah, and Muhammad is the Prophet [or Messenger] of Allah.*

Allah is One, Alone, Absolute, Unique. He has no partners, no intermediaries, no son. This simple statement of faith asserts the importance of Allah as the one Allah and secondary role of Muhammad as the messenger. It is a rejection of polytheism. It makes it clear to a Muslim that there is only one Allah worthy of worship.

As soon as a Muslim says the Shahadah in front of two other Muslims, he or she has made a very solemn declaration and is thereafter expected to follow the teachings and practice of Islam. If an individual with a true and sincere heart makes this first declaration, then he or she will not want this to be merely lip service.

The Shahadah is repeated throughout a Muslim's life. It is the first thing said on awaking and the last thing said when falling asleep. It is whispered into the ear of a newborn Muslim baby and recited at an aqiqah ceremony. An aqiqah ceremony takes place after a baby is born to celebrate the new life and welcome the baby into the family. If possible, it is the last thing heard by a dying person. Without faith in the supremacy of Allah the other duties have little meaning.

Salat

Salat (Salah), the second pillar in Islam, is the name for the mandatory prayers of worship. It is communication with and worship of Allah. Salat, at its deepest level, is personal submission to Allah and to His will followed by praise and worship, which is thanking and adoring Allah for what He is. The Arabic word Salat is difficult to translate adequately into English.

Muslims should perform Salat five times daily. The meaning behind this ritual goes to the heart of Islam. Submission to Allah and to His will is an ongoing process, which is the Muslim way of life. Regular worship builds a stronger relationship with Allah. This is all very necessary because the heart is deceptive, wayward, and prone to wander after temptations. Regular worship in the local mosque also helps. Friendships are formed and one learns about the needs of others in the community.

- **Salat al-fajr**: dawn, before sunrise

- **Salat al-zuhr**: midday, after the sun passes its highest

- **Salat al-'asr**: the late part of the afternoon

- **Salat al-maghrib**: just after sunset

- **Salat al-'isha**: between sunset and midnight

All Muslims try to do this. Muslim children as young as seven are encouraged to pray but it is expected once Muslims reach puberty. Although the salat is not the only form of prayer in Islam, it offers an opportunity to communicate with Allah on a regular basis. It is understood to be a central practice in Islam, as Muhammad said:

Prayer is the pillar of the religion. To neglect it is to prepare the downfall of religion. If a man performs the five prayers in a proper state of purity and at the times prescribed, they will be a light and a proof for him on the day of resurrection.

In most Muslim countries and in some Muslim communities in the UK, each prayer time is announced by the *adhan*, first introduced in Medina by the Prophet. The adhan is traditionally called out from the minarets of mosques and in modern times, often relayed via loudspeakers. As Muhammad proscribed, Muslims still face Mecca to pray. In a mosque, the mihrab marks the direction of prayer. But the word for the direction of Mecca is Qibla. If a person is praying outside a mosque, a compass on a prayer mat can be used to work out the Qibla.

There is no set dress code, but Muslims should wear things that are clean and modest. Technically, Muslims can pray anywhere, but it must be a clean place. Ritual purity. Is achieved through two forms of ablution depending on the circumstance. These are the 'greater ablution' or *ghusl*, and the 'minor ablution', or *wudu.*

The major ablution is required if men have ejaculated or if women have completed menstruation or have given birth; and for both men and women if they have had sexual intercourse. Otherwise, the minor ablution is sufficient.

Wudu includes the washing of the mouth, nose, hands and forearms, face, head, and feet in accordance with the Sunna of the Prophet.

Each prayer is made up of a number of 'units' called *rak'a* which consists of reciting verses from the Qur'an whilst either standing, bowing, and prostration. The rak'a is then repeated until the required number of units – two, three or four, depending on the time of day – is completed.

Those who are unable to pray within the specified times are expected to make up for the loss by offering the prayer later as soon as they are able. Women who are on their period are not allowed to pray until all traces of blood have disappeared.

Zakat

Zakat (or Zakah), or mandatory alms giving, is the third pillar. This follows on naturally from having a strong faith with regular communal worship, because it identifies with the needs of the local community. Religious practice and belief must have an ethical dimension. Taking part in daily ritual practice is pointless if it doesn't affect the relationship people have with those around them.

Linguistically Zakat means to 'purify and grow'. Good Muslims want to aid and support the community in which they live in order to see it prosper. One way to do this is to use the power of financial giving. The amount paid varies depending on the situation of the Muslim. A Muslim who has savings should contribute this to the overall giving of 2.5% of their annual wealth as Zakat.

It is important to remember that Zakat is not charity but an obligation. The rich pay more than those with less money and very poor people pay nothing at all. The *nisab* threshold determines what you need to live on relative to where you live – so no one is going to be put into poverty through this system.

There are strict rules about what can happen with Zakat money. It may only be spent on the poor and needy, Zakat collectors, the purchase of freedom for enslaved people, converts to Islam who are in need, stranded travelers needing help, or anyone in debt.

The method of collecting Zakat varies from individual to individual. In the UK there are many Muslim relief organisations that will collect and distribute the compulsory giving of Zakat, as well as voluntary giving such as Sadaqah.

The meaning or motivation behind such giving is deeply significant. Muslims consider wealth to be a blessing from Allah. Since He values and cares for everyone equally, He naturally expects His blessing and provision to be shared around. Thus, wealth brings with it some form of test or trial. Those who respond by being generous to others enjoy His pleasure and favour, while those who are greedy and self-centered and who hoard wealth, or use it selfishly for themselves, fall into a trap and risk His displeasure. We may deduce from all of this that Zakat is a practical expression of spiritual worship and a religious social security system.

Saum

The fourth pillar is Saum or fasting. Anyone who has fasted prior to a hospital operation, or fasted for a charity in order to help others in need, will realise in a new way the value of food. Anyone who has fasted in order to pray will have discovered the meaning of prayer at a much deeper level too. In Islam, fasting is seen as the duty of all believers.

Qur'an 2:183 O ye who believe! Fasting is prescribed to you as it was prescribed to those before you, that ye may (learn) self-restraint.

The obligatory fasting month lasts for twenty-nine days, i.e. the whole of the lunar month of Ramadan. Between the hours of sunrise and sunset, Muslim adults may have no food or drink. An exemption is permitted for the benefit of the sick, young, old, pregnant or nursing mothers.

The real value of fasting is spiritual, however; it develops discipline, commitment, patience and compassion. It is a spiritual exercise in the giving of obedience to Allah. At the communal level, it is a time for the healing of quarrels by means of forgiveness. It produces empathy and sympathy towards the poor and needy. Morally it strengthens the human will by developing patience and self-control. The celebrations at the end of the month of Ramadan represent a great communal event of the Muslim year worldwide. The poor dine side by side with rulers and leaders on the best food available. Again we see in this feast a demonstration of communal harmony and spiritual commitment.

Hajj

The fifth pillar is the Hajj, the pilgrimage to Mecca (Makkah) in Saudi Arabia. The actual significance of the location dates back many years with some saying that the first Prophet on earth, Adam, built the first Mosque on earth on this location. The second Mosque was the one in Jerusalem.

Muslims must attempt to make a pilgrimage to Mecca (Makkah) once in their lifetime. There are many concessions for those who are unable to do this. Those who are at a mature age and are financially and physically able should strongly consider taking this pilgrimage to purify their soul.

The Hajj signifies the unity of all Muslims, and its general purpose is to cleanse the heart before Allah and to unite all Muslims. Muslim men and women all take part in this international ritual practice that brings together Muslims from all parts of the globe.

For the average pilgrim Hajj is an overwhelming and unforgettable experience, the greatest of his life. It is seen as a victory over race, language, and national differences. Pilgrims all look alike, wearing sleeveless garments made from white cotton, regardless of their personal rank, wealth or role in society. These clothes are referred to as *ihram*, however the 'state of ihram' is not just about the correct clothing, one must be ritually cleansed. For men, this means cutting the hair and shaving. During the pilgrimage men and women must wash with water but not soap - and perfume is forbidden.

The Hajj properly begins with the *tawaf* which consists of walking around the *ka'ba* anticlockwise seven times. Many pilgrims will also try to kiss the 'black stone'. There are usually so many pilgrims that getting close to the ka'ba is impossible, and pilgrims will circle it at a distance.

Once the tawaf is over, pilgrims then perform the *sa'i*. This involves rushing (or walking at speed) between the two small hills of Safa and Marwa. This is to emulate the trials of Hagar, the mother of Isma'il, who after being abandoned in the desert by Abraham had to search for water to quench her son's third. God revealed the Zamzam well to save they, and Pilgrims complete the sa'i by drinking from it.

At midday the pilgrims move to Mina where they remain until the next morning until they move on to the plain of Arafat to set up camp. They then proceed with the *wuquf* or 'standing' when they call upon Allah to forgive them. This goes on from noon until sunset and ended with a sermon. It is said that upon completing this act, Muslims are as sinless as the day that they were born.

At sunset the pilgrims move their camp to Muzdalifa where they must also collect pebbles for the next day. At sunrise, the pilgrims move back to Mina to perform a ritual of 'stoning the devil.' This involves throwing small pebbles at three stone pillars that symbolise Satan and his evil ways.

Once this is over, pilgrims who have the financial means to do so are encouraged to sacrifice a sheep, goat or camel. This is to recognise Abraham's trial in which God had commanded him to kill his son, but later provided an animal in his place.

It is then recommended that male pilgrims shave their heads and females have a few centimeters of their hair trimmed.

Whilst on Hajj everyone should be gentle, respectful, and tolerant towards others and this should lead to stronger relationships, which are strengthened by peace and forgiveness. The spirit of Hajj is the spirit of total sacrifice: sacrifice of personal comforts, worldly pleasures, wealth, companionship of relatives and friends, varieties of dress and personal appearance, pride, work, or social status. During pilgrimage Muslims must stop all sexual contact, shedding of blood, hunting, uprooting of plants, cutting nails and shaving. The whole pilgrimage is designed to lead the pilgrim to a state where he can resist the tricks of the Evil One, and so fully dedicate his life to Allah.

Conclusion

Having briefly outlined the Five Pillars of Islam, it should be noted that such observations are considered to represent the minimal obligations in Islam. They are an overview of faith in practice, and not the whole religion. Taqwa, the consciousness or awareness of Allah, should permeate the whole of life, and not just the rituals. Ishan is another important aspect of belief, which is to believe and act in the remembrance of Allah and in closeness with Him. If a Muslim was to do all of this, then the Five Pillars would fit quite well into a Muslim life without them being seen as a chore or duty.

Nonetheless, the proper observance of the Five Pillars does have definite value. They help to 'straighten' the person out, spiritually speaking, before Allah. A proper application of the Five Pillars can enable the Muslim to begin to function as Allah's deputy here on earth, and so prepare for the world to come.

6 SUBMISSION

The word 'Islam' in Arabic translates to the English word 'submission'. It is not meant to be a name or title, but rather a description. A Muslim is literally 'one who submits'.

True submission is only possible when Muslim's realise that they only exist because of their Creator – Allah. Life is purely 'on loan' and should be 'given back' to its rightful Owner. This is achieved through living life in accordance to Allah's Will.

The Muslim practice of submission involves following the commandments and teachings of the Qur'an, and the example set by the Prophet Muhammad. But ultimately, it involves surrendering oneself to Allah and accepting His guidance and direction. It means acknowledging Allah's supremacy and recognizing that He along has power and control over all things in the universe.

Muslims practice submission through various acts of worship, including daily prayers, fasting during the month of Ramadan, giving charity, and performing the pilgrimage to Mecca. But it also involves adhering to moral and ethical codes of conduct, such as being honest, just, kind, and merciful.

The spiritual journey set out in the Qur'an, is one in which humans attempt to mirror God's attributes. This is not to say they should attempt to be 'like' Allah or to compare themselves to him. But rather, it means letting go of ideas of personal ownership or autonomy, and seeking purely to be a mirror of God's perfection.

Overall, the practice of submission in Islam is a way of life that emphasizes the importance of humility, compassion, and devotion to Allah. It is a means of achieving inner peace and being in harmony with the world around us.

Ibadah is an Arabic term that refers to the worship or devotion that Muslims offer to Allah. It is a fundamental concept in Islam and encompasses all acts of obedience and submission to Allah. For Muslims, ibadah is a way of life and a means of attaining closeness to Allah and earning His pleasure. It is not merely a ritualistic practice but a spiritual journey of self-discipline, self-improvement, and moral purification. Through ibadah, Muslims seek to develop a deeper connection with Allah, strengthen their faith, and fulfil their purpose in life.

The moment Muslims 'open their eyes' and become conscious of Allah, they must obey Allah's commands in full. This awareness is known as *Taqwa*. Taqwa alters the entire motivation for doing kind or good deeds. One is not kind, or thoughtful, or generous because 'it pays' (obliging others to return the favour), but because one is living as Allah intended – as his vice regent who cares for the whole of the created order.

Living with Allah at the forefront of their minds is called Ihsan. Muhammad referred to Ihsan as follows:

Ishan is to worship Allah as if you are seeing Him, for He sees you even if you do not see Him.

This faith should be a constant motivation to do good works throughout the whole of one's life. This is why Muslims believe that Islam is a way of life and cannot be separated from any part of their daily life – whether social, economic or political. Faith and good works are a pleasure that only increases pleasure, as a stone thrown sends ripples across a pond. They are not a burden or cause of fear.

To fear Allah means to respect, honour and worship Allah as there being no other god or anything else equal or superior to Allah. This means Muslims want to do and live their best for fear of dishonouring Allah. Also thinking ahead to judgement.

7 WORSHIP: PRAYER; MOSQUE

Prayer

In addition to five daily prayers (the *salat*), believers are free to talk to God and call on Him whenever they wish. Non-obligatory prayers of this kind are known as *du'a* which literally means to 'call on' God. So whilst *salat* is seen as a form of public worship, the spiritual exercise *du'a* is private worship. These may be offered at any time and in any place, depending on the needs of the individual. Ritual cleansing is not necessary, and women are allowed to offer du'a during their period. Muslims may also recite the 99 names of Allah using a string of 33 or 99 beads to help them pray.

Communal prayer

Jummah is congregational prayer held on a Friday just after noon at the mosque. Praying together as a community is meant to develop the feeling of unity among the Muslim community.

The imam gives two sermons or *khutbar* and a series of *rak'as* are performed. Men are obliged to go to Friday midday prayers (Jummah) except if they are ill or too old to attend.

Women do not have to go to Friday prayers at the mosque and instead may choose to pray at home. All that is needed is a clean place to pray so that they can show proper respect for Allah. The mother's role is important in teaching children prayers and readings from the Qur'an.

The Mosque

The mosque is commonly understood to be the Muslim place of worship, although they can be housed in any type of building, those that are purpose built share a number of common features.

- Minaret: this is a tall, slender tower that is usually located at one corner of the mosque. Traditionally, the muezzin would sin the call to prayer form here, however now there is often a loudspeaker at the top of the spire.

- Dome: a large, rounded roof that covers the main prayer hall. In hot countries, this is intended to help keep the hall cool to avoid people sweating during prayer and becoming unclean.

- Prayer hall: this is the main area of the mosque where Muslims gather to prayer. It is usually a large, open space with no chairs or pews. It often has a padded carpet so that Muslims are able to pray in public. Many mosques have a separate area for women to pray so that people are no distracted by the opposite gender. Where this is not possible, women pray at the back of the hall.

- Qibla wall: this is the wall that faces towards the Kaaba in mecca, which is the direction that Muslims face during prayer as commanded by Allah.

- Mihrab: a niche in the qibla wall that indicates the direction of Mecca. It is usually decorated with intricate patterns and calligraphy with verses from the Qu'ran. These are meant to reflect the beauty of Islamic art and design. There must be no depiction of Allah or Muhammad.

- Minbar: this is a raised platform from where the Imam (leader of prayers) delivers his sermon.

- Wudu area: a designated area for Muslims to perform ablution (ritual washing) before prayer so that they are clean before greeting Allah in prayer.

- Courtyard: an open space outside the mosque where people can gather for community events or social gatherings.

Verses from the Qur'an in various styles of calligraphy are often displayed in the home as decoration, but as in the mosque, there are no images of Allah or the Prophet Muhammad.
Some homes have a *qiblah* to show the direction of Makkah (Mecca).

Even at home, Muslims must perform wudu before prayers, take off their shoes and use a prayer mat. They perform several rak'as of *Salat* facing Makkah.

The Qur'an teaches that the whole world is a mosque, so people can pray anywhere. The important thing for Muslims is to keep

Allah constantly in mind by worshipping him five times daily.

The role of the Mosque

One of the mosque's roles is to provide a place for worship: at the mosque people are called to prayer by the muezzin, sometimes from a minaret which is a tall spire which the muezzin would traditionally sing from, however now this is often a loudspeaker at the top of the spire on a mosque.

Once everyone has followed wudu (ritual washing), the Imam leads the people in rak'ahs (prayer movements) at Jumma (Friday prayer). However, Muslims' are welcome to pray any of the Salah prayers at the mosque throughout the day.

Mosaics with complicated patterns decorate many mosques, but there are no images of Allah, Muhammad or any other human or animal figures. Allah is considered to be beyond human understanding and therefore cannot be portrayed. Pictures or statues of other human figures are avoided because they could mistakenly be worshipped, which would be idolotry or shirk, which is one of the gravest sins in Islam.

Instead, calligraphy is often used to decorate the walls of the mosque with important passages from the Qur'an.

The mosque's role here is two-fold, it needs to provide the congregation with a place to pray with all the facilities needed e.g. washing facilities or a qibla showing the direction of Mecca. But by providing Muslims with the opportunity to worship without distraction, members of the congregation can not only improve their relationship with Allah but also feel a sense of community by gathering to pray with others.

Education

For worship to be meaningful, it needs to be understood:

During Friday prayer the Imam may give a khutbah (sermon). This 'khutbah' provides guidance in Islamic teaching. The East London Mosque puts these online each week for those unable to attend in person.

Many mosques also provide classes for children and young people. They teach Muslim children subjects such as Arabic to recite the Qur'an and lessons in the principles and practices of their faith, such as the five pillars.

This shows that the role of the mosque is to help believers understand their faith, and not to just practice blindly. By doing this from such a young age, Muslims can grow up secure in their knowledge. With this understanding and education, the mosque provides the opportunity for Muslims to become closer to Allah as they will have a greater understanding of everything He has done for them and provided.

Community centre

The mosque also provides opportunities for the community to gather for a range of events: for example, Muslims can announce weddings, as Muhammad advised "announce the wedding ceremonies, hold them in mosques, and make them known by beating the drums."

Also, many activities that aren't necessarily linked to religion are also held in mosques such as Scout groups, fitness classes, school tuition and CV-writing workshops.

This shows that the role of the Mosque is also to build a community filled with like-minded people with the same beliefs. This could help Muslims because they know that if they were to ever struggle with faith, they have a community around them who would be able to help.

Ultimately, by experiencing day to day life surrounded by other Muslims, it may be easier to maintain Ishan (keeping Allah at forefront of mind), and to practice ibadah (life as an act of worship).

8 CONFLICT

Types of War

There are several types of war, which can be categorized based on different factors such as nature, objective, participants, or tactics. To list them all would almost be exhaustive, but they can be broadly categorised as follows:

1. Conventional War: Traditional warfare involving the use of regular military forces, tactics, and weapons, such as tanks, aircraft, and infantry.

2. Guerrilla War: A type of asymmetric warfare where a smaller, less organized, and often local group uses hit-and-run tactics, ambushes, and sabotage against a larger, conventional force.

3. Civil War: An armed conflict between factions within a country, where different groups within the same nation fight for control or independence.

4. World War: This a large-scale conflict that involves multiple nations or regions across different continents and affects a significant portion of the world's population. It is characterized by the extensive mobilization of military forces, widespread destruction, and global impact.

5. Cyber War: A form of warfare that takes place in the digital realm, where nations or groups engage in offensive or defensive operations using computer networks and information systems.

6. Nuclear War: A type of warfare that involves the use of nuclear weapons, with the potential for catastrophic and widespread destruction.

It's important to note that these types of wars are not always mutually exclusive, and conflicts can often involve elements from multiple categories.

Case Study: World Wars

The term "world war" originated from its association with the two major conflicts of the 20th century: World War I (1914-1918) and World War II (1939-1945). These wars involved numerous countries and resulted in the loss of millions of lives and significant geopolitical changes.

A world war typically arises from complex combinations of political, economic, territorial, and ideological disputes between nations. It often begins with a single event or series of events that escalate tensions and trigger a chain reaction of alliances and military actions. The conflicts typically involve both conventional and unconventional warfare, including battles on land, sea, and air, as well as strategic bombing, naval blockades, and large-scale troop deployments.

World War II is perhaps the most notable of the two world wars due to both its length and the subsequent casualty rate; an estimated 80 million killed. It was fought between two major military alliances of the allies (France, USA, UK etc) and the axis (Germany, Italy, Japan etc). It is clear to see this war as a world war not only due to the various forces involved in this war but also the scale over which it was fought. War simultaneously broke out in the far east with the Japanese invasion of China and many French and UK territories such as Singapore and in Europe with the Nazi invasion of Poland and eventually France. Due to the nature of the colonial powers involved in this war war quickly spread into colonies in Africa and Asia. The technological advances and weaponry around this time were also responsible for making this war the most destructive in history with weapons such as the atomic bomb having their first and last use in conflict in the bombings of Hiroshima and Nagasaki.

Moral Issues Arising from World Wars

One moral issue arising from World Wars is that it brings about a huge number of casualties. This is a fact. Approximately 80 million people were killed during World War II. To analyse this fact, you need to think about the consequences of those deaths. For example, it is estimated that around 50% of these deaths were civilians – should they have been dragged into a war that they did not choose to fight?

It is hard not to think of the Holocaust in relation to World War II. Whilst this too raises the question of whether it is right to kill someone, it further raises moral questions about the responsibility of individuals and nations in preventing and addressing such crimes.

Case Study: Civil War

A civil war is an armed conflict that occurs within a single country, typically between different factions or groups within that country. It is characterized by internal struggles for power, control over territory, or ideological differences. Unlike international wars, which involve conflicts between separate nations, civil wars take place within the borders of a single state.

A notable recent example of a civil war is the 2014 Syrian Civil War. This war began as part of the 2011 Arab Spring in which nations throughout the Middle East took part in peaceful protests to try and establish regime changes. As protests in Syria were met with growing resistance from Basher al-Assad's government the protests grew into pockets of violence and eventually a large-scale war. The most notable opposition force to the Assad government was the Free Syrian Army, but many other groups grew in power vacuums left by the conflict. This included Kurdish rebels and ISIS in the north of Syria. In 2015 Assad's main ally, Putin's Russia, joined the conflict with military support. This escalation of violence led to a major refugee crisis across the Middle East and Europe.

Moral Issues Arising from Civil War

The Syrian civil war has resulted in immense human suffering, with millions of people internally displaced or forced to flee as refugees. The conflict has caused significant destruction of infrastructure, including hospitals, schools, and residential areas. It has also witnessed the use of chemical weapons, indiscriminate bombings, and other war crimes, leading to widespread condemnation from the international community.

Efforts to resolve the Syrian civil war have been challenging, with numerous failed ceasefires and peace negotiations. Multiple factions with competing interests, the involvement of external powers, and the rise of extremist groups have made finding a comprehensive solution extremely difficult.

Case Study: Cyber War

Cyber war refers to the use of cyber attacks and digital tactics by nation-states or other entities to disrupt, damage, or gain control over the information systems and infrastructure of another nation-state. It involves the deliberate and systematic exploitation of vulnerabilities in computer networks, software, and hardware to achieve strategic objectives. In a cyber war, the primary targets are often critical infrastructure systems, such as power grids, transportation networks, financial systems, military communication networks, and government databases. By infiltrating and compromising these systems, attackers can cause significant disruption, economic damage, and even loss of life.

One example of a cyber war is the Stuxnet attack, which is widely believed to be a joint effort by the United States and Israel against Iran's nuclear program. Stuxnet was a highly sophisticated computer worm that targeted industrial control systems, specifically those used in Iran's nuclear facilities.

In 2010, Stuxnet infected Iran's nuclear infrastructure, causing significant damage to its uranium enrichment centrifuges. The worm was designed to exploit vulnerabilities in the control systems and manipulate the speed of the centrifuges, leading to their destruction or rendering them inoperable. This covert cyber operation aimed to disrupt Iran's nuclear program without resorting to traditional military action.

Moral Issues Arising from Cyber War

The Stuxnet attack demonstrated the potential of cyber warfare as a means to achieve strategic objectives. It highlighted the growing significance of cyber capabilities in modern warfare, showcasing the ability to target critical infrastructure and disrupt key systems. However, the attack also raised concerns about the potential for escalation and the blurred lines between traditional warfare and cyber warfare.

In cyber wars, there is a risk of unintended consequences, such as disrupting civilian infrastructure or causing harm to non-targeted individuals. The ethical concern lies in minimizing harm to innocent parties and ensuring proportional responses.

Identifying the perpetrators of cyber attacks and holding them accountable can be challenging due to the anonymous nature of cyberspace. This raises moral questions about the responsibility of states, organizations, and individuals in preventing and responding to cyber warfare.

Finally, Cyber warfare lacks well-established ethical norms and rules of engagement as compared to traditional warfare.

Establishing international agreements and protocols that balance national security interests with the protection of civilians and critical infrastructure is a moral challenge.

Religious Viewpoints: Just War Theory

Just war theories have existed since ancient Egypt in some form or other but over the centuries has become a Christian tradition of judging both the morality of going to war and the morality of how wars should be fought. The two most important thinkers in developing the Christian JWT are St Augustine and St Aquinas.

The concept of Just War in Catholicism is a set of principles and criteria that guide the moral evaluation of warfare. It provides a framework for determining when the use of force is morally justified and the conditions under which military action can be considered legitimate.

Just War Theory consists of eight criteria by which a war can be judged to be just (fair/right).

When it is right to fight (Jus ad Bellum – Justice _of_ war)

- War can only be embarked upon for a just cause i.e. invasion or threat of invasion, violation of a treaty, in support of an ally against an aggressor.
- The war must be declared by lawful authorities. The war must be declared by lawful authorities means that the rightful government or ruler must make an official declaration of war.
- It must be embarked upon with right intention. The only desirable outcome of war is a just peace. Vengeance or empire building is not right intention.
- It must be the last resort. War must only be declared after all alternatives have been exhausted e.g. negotiations, economic sanctions.

- There must be proportionality. The good to be accomplished must be greater than the evil consequences of the war.
- There must be a reasonable probability of success. Unless there is a good chance of success then the destruction caused will be unlikely to lead to a just outcome i.e. better than if the war had never been fought.

How war should be fought (jus in bello – Justice _in_ war)

- Proportionality. Excessive force must never be deployed. The amount of destructive force used must be no more than is necessary to achieve the peace desired.
- Discrimination. Immunity of non-combatants and moderation must be practiced. Care should be taken to avoid killing or injuring civilians, causalities, medical staff and prisoners of war. At the cessation of hostilities the enemy must be treated with charity and justice not vengeance.

Applying Just War Theory to World War

The question of whether a specific war, such as World War I or World War II, can be justified according to the just war theory is a complex: whilst theory provides a set of principles and criteria to evaluate the moral legitimacy of a war, ultimately, the application of these principles is subjective and can lead to differing interpretations.

In the case of World War I, for example, proponents of the just war theory argue that the war could be justified based on the principles of self-defence and the protection of innocent lives. The assassination of Archduke Franz Ferdinand of Austria-Hungary, which triggered the war, was seen as an act of aggression that threatened the stability and security of various nations. Additionally, the defence of smaller nations against the expansionist ambitions of larger powers could be seen as a just cause.

Similarly, in the case of World War II, the aggression of Nazi Germany and its allies, including the Holocaust and other grave human rights violations, is often cited as a just cause for war. The restoration of justice, defence of innocent lives, and the prevention of further atrocities were considered morally imperative.

Non-Religious Viewpoint: Kant

Immanuel Kant was a German philosopher who is most well known for his deontological ethical theory. Deontology is a rules based ethics system where right and wrong is determined not by things like the outcome of our actions, but upon our obedience to rules. Quite simply an action is right if it follows the rules and wrong if it breaks it. None of this is ground breaking but what is different about Kant is the way he came to deciding what his rules should be. He was an atheist, so didn't depend on moral codes like the 10 commandments. Instead he built his rules on something we all have reason. Our reason will help us determine right from wrong as we are able to then consider things like our intentions, and what our duty should be in any instance when dealing with other rational beings. With this in mind he wrote two Categorical Imperatives. These are moral principles that should be followed in all places and at all times by all people.

1. "Act only upon that maxim, which at the same time you can will to become a universal law"

   This is called the **Universalisability Test**. In other words, could I logically wish for others, in the same situation, to do what I am about to do?

2. "Act in such a way that you always treat humanity, whether in your own person or in the person of any other, never simply as a means, but always at the same time as an end."

   This is called the **Ends in Themselves Test**. In other words, if I do this, will I be using people as a means to an end or will I be respecting their humanity?

Applying Kant to Types of War

1. For Kantians, the key objection to warfare is the fact that all wars inevitably cause the death of innocents – a decision to go to war is therefore a decision to sacrifice innocents. This treats human beings as expendable commodities and violates the Kantian requirement that people are never used as means to an end but treated as ends in themselves.
2. Kant argued that people – unlike animals – have reason. People are not subject to the "mechanical plays of nature" and should, therefore, be able to solve their differences by "mode of a civil process".
3. Using reason, man can discover that it is a categorical imperative to strive for perpetual peace, whether or not it can be achieved. However, by striving for genuine peace, we may achieve a "continuous approximation" of it.
4. Kant anticipated the destruction that would be caused by modern warfare. He suggested that, if we continue to resolve disputes by force, we will eventually achieve peace in "The great graveyard of the human race" after a war of extermination.

Kant also argued that the "constant readiness to fight" (i.e. being prepared for war), in order to deter aggression, actually encourages other nations to make the same preparations. This preparation for war can actually be the cause of conflict.

Justifications for War

In essence, justifications for war refer to the reasons or arguments put forth to justify the use of military force by a nation or group. These justifications aim to provide moral, legal, or strategic reasons for engaging in armed conflict. Each justification can vary depending on the specific circumstances, political motivations, and international legal framework:

1. Self-defence: The most widely accepted justification for war is self-defence. This principle asserts that a nation has the right to defend itself against an imminent or ongoing aggression that threatens its security or the safety of its citizens. Under this justification, the use of force is seen as a last resort and proportionate response to protect one's own interests.

2. Humanitarian intervention: In certain cases, war has been justified as a means to protect or assist a population facing severe human rights abuses or genocide. Advocates argue that intervention is necessary to prevent or halt mass atrocities and save lives. However, the ethical and legal aspects of humanitarian intervention are heavily debated, as it involves intervening in the internal affairs of another state.

3. Pre-emptive strike: Some argue for war as a pre-emptive measure to prevent an imminent attack or to dismantle a potential threat. This justification rests on the belief that acting before an adversary can strike is necessary to protect national security. However, the pre-emptive use of force is highly

controversial, as it raises concerns about the legality and proportionality of the action.

4. National interest: Realpolitik justifications argue that war may be justified in pursuit of national interests, such as protecting economic resources, ensuring territorial integrity, or advancing geopolitical goals. Critics argue that this justification can be easily manipulated and may lead to conflict based on self-interest rather than ethical considerations.

5. Alliances: an alliance is an association of nations or groups formed together in order to advance common interest or cause. These alliances can result in war firstly because if a single ally is drawn into a conflict then the others may be obliged to support their ally.

Case Study: Pre-emptive Strikes

The 1968 Six-Day War fought between Israel and an alliance of its neighbours (Egypt, Jordan, Iraq and Syria) is one of the most successful pre-emptive strikes in history. Israel believed that war with its neighbours as their military forces grew around its borders. As they were outmatched on paper they planned a massive offensive before an invasion could begin. This was predominantly achieved through efficient airstrikes on enemy airfields in order to achieve dominance of the surrounding airspace. With the airspace secured Israel's ground offensive could make great progress, pushing Egypt back across the Sinai peninsula all the way to the Suez canal. The war lasted only six days as Israel secured a swift victory. Israel only suffered around 800 however there opposing alliances suffered estimated losses of around 15,000.

Moral issues with Pre-emptive Strikes

the most obvious concern with pre-emptive strikes is that they are based upon assumption. If a nation is correct in assuming they will be attacked then pre-emptive strikes not only increase the chance of victory but also reduce the number of casualties experienced. However it is easy to misunderstand the intentions of another nation and as a result become the real aggressor of the conflict. Military exercises often involve movements of large troop numbers and these may only be intended as a show of force but in fact lead to war.

Another concern is the manner in which attacks are launched at targets not yet involved in conflict. As it is easier to neutralise an enemy aircraft whilst it is on the ground, pre-emptive strikes will result in attacking airbases of nations which are not at war this will increase the risk of killing innocents on the ground and to some extent even military personnel in these airbases may be seen as innocent as they themselves are not aware that they are involved in a conflict.

Case Study: Alliances

World War I is one such war more or less caused by growing alliances. In the late 19th century and alliance between Germany, Austro Hungary and Italy was formed (the triple alliance) which resulted in the formation of the triple entente, and alliance between France, Russia and the UK. As these two alliances green power war became more inevitable and 1914 war broke out after a complicated set of circumstances led to each alliance being dragged further and further into conflict. The war lasted for four years and resulted in the death of around 21 million people.

Moral issues with Alliances

The first issue is that alliances are often like a self-fulfilling prophecy. Nations enter the alliances in order to prevent more and deter aggression, but this may be seen as an aggressive move by any opposing alliance. This means that in efforts to create and maintain peace nations are in fact only growing tensions to create war.

A second moral issue with alliances is that any ensuing war will often be larger in scale. It is no surprise that both world wars were fought between major alliances. Conflicts which might have been resolved with small skirmishes between one or two nations are grown into enormous conflict fought between powerful and populous nations and as a result more civilians can be put in harm's way.

Religious Viewpoint: Christian Pacifism

Pacifism is opposition to war, militarism or violence. The word pacifism was coined by the French peace campaigner Émile Arnaud and adopted by other peace activists at the tenth Universal Peace Congress in Glasgow in 1901. Pacifism is found in many of  the worlds major faiths and many non-religious people also hold pacifist views. Christian pacifism however is when people choose to adopt a pacifist position on war due to their Christian beliefs. They hold the view that much of the bible and life of Jesus suggests that complete non-violence is the only moral approach to conflict.

Christian Pacifist Quotes

Exodus 20:13 'Thou shalt not kill.'

Luke 22

47 While he was still speaking a crowd came up, and the man who was called Judas, one of the Twelve, was leading them. He approached Jesus to kiss him, 48 but Jesus asked him, "Judas, are you betraying the Son of Man with a kiss?"49 When Jesus' followers saw what was going to happen, they said, "Lord, should we strike with our swords?" 50 And one of them struck the servant of the high priest, cutting off his right ear.51 But Jesus answered, "No more of this!" And he touched the man's ear and healed him.52 Then Jesus said to the chief priests, the officers of the temple guard, and the elders, who had come for him, "Am I leading a rebellion, that you have come with swords and clubs? 53 Every day I was with you in the temple courts, and you did not lay a hand on me. But this is your hour—when darkness reigns.

Matthew 5

38 "You have heard that it was said, 'Eye for eye, and tooth for tooth.'[a] 39 But I tell you, do not resist an evil person. If anyone slaps you on the right cheek, turn to them the other cheek also. 40 And if anyone wants to sue you and take your shirt, hand over your coat as well. 41 If anyone forces you to go one mile, go with them two miles. 42 Give to the one who asks you, and do not turn away from the one who wants to borrow from you.

43 "You have heard that it was said, 'Love your neighbour[b] and hate your enemy.' 44 But I tell you, love your enemies and pray for those who persecute you, 45 that you may be children of your Father in heaven. He causes his sun to rise on the evil and the good, and sends rain on the righteous and the unrighteous. 46 If you love those who love you, what reward will you get? Are not even the tax collectors doing that? 47 And if you greet only your own people, what are you doing more than others? Do not even pagans do that? 48 Be perfect, therefore, as your heavenly Father is perfect.

Applying Christian Pacifism to Justifications of War

As Christian pacifism is primarily rooted in Jesus' teachings of love, forgiveness, and turning the other cheek. Many Christian pacifists advocate for alternative approaches to war, such as non-violent resistance or diplomatic negotiations, even in the face of aggression. Therefore they would conclude there is no justification for war.

Non-Religious Viewpoint: Utilitarianism

Utilitarianism is a consequentialist moral theory of ethics which is widely attributed to Jeremy Bentham and J.S Mill. Bentham believed that all human beings are governed by two things, pleasure and pain, he felt that the reasons for any person's actions could be reduced to either their pursuit of pleasure or their avoidance of pain. Upon this he based his principle of utility – "An action is right if it produces the greatest happiness for the greatest number." We should seek to estimate what pleasures and what pains may be created by our actions and to preform the action that will produce the most pleasure. It is also important to note that utilitarianism is an egalitarian theory and so every person including ourselves must be given equal value in any moral calculation. Finally the true morality of our action will be discovered once we perform our action, this means that even if we intend good from our actions the moral worth will only be found in its outcome and sadly this may not always be as we predicted.

Applying Utilitarianism to Justifications of War

The utilitarian would view each war independently. They don't focus on whether war goes against certain moral rules, like 'never harm innocent people.' Instead, they look at whether war will lead to certain outcomes. If a war brings more happiness than unhappiness overall, then, according to the principle of utility, it is morally acceptable. So, when deciding if a defensive or offensive war against country B is morally right, it all depends on whether the benefits for country A are greater than the suffering of those who are killed, injured, or lose loved ones. Whatever this benefit may be, it is considered justified to harm innocent people if it adds to the overall happiness of everyone.

Alternatives to war

Alternatives to war are nonviolent means of resolving conflicts and achieving goals. Here are some common alternatives:

1. Diplomacy and negotiation: Diplomatic efforts, such as negotiation, mediation, and dialogue, can be effective ways of resolving conflicts without resorting to war. This involves engaging in discussions to find mutually acceptable solutions and compromises.

2. International institutions and organizations: Utilizing international institutions, such as the United Nations, can provide a platform for peaceful dispute resolution. These organizations can facilitate negotiations, provide mediation services, and promote dialogue between conflicting parties.

3. Economic and trade measures: Economic and trade sanctions, embargoes, and boycotts can be used as alternative strategies to influence the behaviour of nations or deter aggression, without resorting to military force.

4. Peacekeeping and peacebuilding: Deploying international peacekeeping forces can help stabilize conflict zones and create an environment conducive to peace negotiations. Additionally, peacebuilding efforts aim to address the root causes of conflicts and build sustainable peace by fostering reconciliation, promoting development, and strengthening institutions.

5. Humanitarian aid and development assistance: Providing humanitarian aid and development assistance to countries or regions facing conflicts can address underlying socio-economic

issues, alleviate suffering, and contribute to long-term stability and peace.

6. Legal measures: Utilizing international law and legal mechanisms, such as tribunals and courts, can help hold accountable those responsible for war crimes or human rights violations. This can contribute to justice and reconciliation while avoiding armed conflict.

Case Study: Sanctions

A recent example of the use of sanctions are those used against Russia after their invasion of Ukraine. These sanctions date back to 2014 when Russia annexed the Crimean peninsula. At this time they were targeted at Russia's ruling elite (the Oligarchs) when many nations and groups like the EU froze all of these high value individual's assets held abroad. This aimed to exert power over the Kremlin by pressuring those closest to Putin. These sanctions were extended in February 2022 when the full scale invasion of Ukraine began. Several companies such as MacDonalds withdrew from Russia and they were expelled from the SWIFT banking system (the system that banks use to exchange currencies across the world).

Moral issues with Sanctions

A first issue with sanctions is that they can have a serious detrimental impact on the civilian population of a country. As sanctions are designed to impact economies, it can lead to rising levels of poverty and unemployment. Furthermore, some sanctions have led to issues with supply of non-sanctioned goods such as medicines. Sanctions placed on Iran, banned the sale of many goods to Iran, so companies became concerned that if they were found in violation of sanctions, they may be punished themselves, rather than risk being caught fowl of the law they simply chose to avoid all business with Iran.

Another major concern is regarding the effectiveness of sanctions unless every nation chooses to uphold them. There are nations in the world who have no real concern with violating sanctions as they may have nothing to lose. In the Ukraine conflict, many of the weapons supplied to Russia have been from North Korea and Iran, both nations already sanctioned by the West.

Case Study: Diplomacy and Negotiation

Following the end of apartheid in South Africa, the Truth and Reconciliation Commission (TRC) was established in 1996. The TRC provided a forum for victims and perpetrators to share their experiences and offered amnesty to those who confessed to human rights violations committed during apartheid. Through public hearings, the TRC aimed to promote healing, reconciliation, and societal transformation, acknowledging the importance of truth-telling and justice without resorting to widespread violence.

Moral issues with Diplomacy and Negotiation

One moral issue is the question of justice and accountability for human rights violations and war crimes. Alternatives to war, such as negotiated settlements or truth and reconciliation processes, may involve granting amnesty or leniency to perpetrators in exchange for peace. This raises concerns about whether justice is being served and whether victims' rights are being adequately addressed.

Peace agreements often require compromise and concessions from all parties involved. This can lead to moral dilemmas when certain compromises involve sacrificing fundamental rights, territorial claims, or the interests of marginalized groups. Decisions made in the pursuit of peace may raise questions about the ethical trade-offs involved and the potential long-term consequences.

Non-religious viewpoint: The United Nations

The United Nations (UN) is an intergovernmental organization that aims to maintain international peace and security, develop friendly relations among nations, achieve international cooperation, and be a centre for harmonizing the actions of nations. The UN is headquartered on international territory in New York City, with its other main offices in Geneva, Nairobi, Vienna, and The Hague.

The UN was established after World War II with the aim of preventing future wars, succeeding the ineffective League of Nations. In1945, 50 governments met and started drafting the UN Charter. This is the agreement that all nations who wish to join the UN must agree and abide by. The organization's objectives include maintaining international peace and security, protecting human rights, delivering humanitarian aid, promoting sustainable development, and upholding international law. At its founding, the UN had 51 member states; with the addition of South Sudan in 2011, membership is now 193, representing almost all of the world's sovereign states.

The Security Council

The United Nations Security Council is one of the six principal organs of the UN, charged with ensuring international peace and security, recommending the admission of new UN members to the General Assembly, and approving any changes to the UN Charter. Its powers include establishing peacekeeping operations, enacting international sanctions, and authorizing military action. The UNSC is the only UN body with the authority to issue binding resolutions on member states.

The Security Council consists of fifteen members, of which five are permanent: China, France, Russia, the United Kingdom, and the United States of America. These were the

great powers, or their successor states, that were the victors of World War II. Permanent members can veto any resolution, including those on the admission of new member states to the United Nations. The remaining ten members are elected on a regional basis to serve a term of two years.

Resolutions of the Security Council are typically enforced by UN peacekeepers, military forces voluntarily provided by member states and funded independently of the main UN budget. As of March 2019, there are thirteen peacekeeping missions with over 81,000 personnel from 121 countries, with a total budget of nearly $6.7 billion.

Applying the UN to Alternatives to War

It should almost go without saying that the United Nations (UN) strongly promotes alternatives to war and advocates for peaceful resolutions of conflicts whenever possible. The UN Charter, which serves as the organization's foundational document, emphasizes the central importance of maintaining international peace and security.

One of the primary mechanisms the UN employs to address conflicts is through diplomacy and negotiation. The UN encourages member states to engage in peaceful dialogue, mediation, and diplomatic efforts to resolve disputes. The organization facilitates negotiations through various bodies like the Security Council, General Assembly, and specialized agencies.

The UN also supports and promotes non-violent conflict resolution methods, such as mediation, arbitration, and reconciliation processes. It provides resources, expertise, and logistical support to parties engaged in negotiations, helping to foster peaceful settlements.

Additionally, the UN upholds the principles of international law, including humanitarian law and human rights law, as essential tools for resolving conflicts and preventing the escalation of violence. Through its various agencies and peacekeeping operations, the UN works to protect civilians, promote human rights, and support peacebuilding efforts in conflict-affected regions.

Overall, the UN views alternatives to war as fundamental in maintaining global peace and stability, and it actively encourages and supports non-violent approaches to conflict resolution.

Non-Religious Rules of War

The Geneva Conventions are a set of four treaties established in 1949 which aim to govern the actions of nations and individuals in war. These treaties would be important for both the UN who would always look to uphold them and sanction those who break them and a Rule Utilitarian who would see them as rules which seek to create the "greatest amount of pleasure for the greatest number of people". The Geneva Conventions extensively define the basic rights of wartime prisoners (civilians and military personnel), establish protections for the wounded and sick, and protections for the civilians in and around a war-zone.

The Conventions

The First Geneva Convention

The Geneva Convention for the Improvement of the Condition of the Wounded and Sick in Armed Forces in the Field. The First Geneva Convention protects soldiers who are **hors de combat** (out of the battle). Including

- Wounded and sick soldiers
- Medical personnel, facilities and equipment
- Wounded and sick civilian support personnel accompanying the armed forces
- Military chaplains
- Civilians who spontaneously take up arms to repel an invasion

Specific provisions include:

Art. 12 The wounded and sick shall be respected and protected without discrimination on the basis of sex, race, nationality, religion, political beliefs or other criteria.

Art. 12 The wounded and sick shall not be murdered, exterminated or subjected to torture or biological experiments.

Art. 15 The wounded and sick shall receive adequate care.

Art. 15 The wounded and sick shall be protected against pillage and ill treatment.

The Second Geneva Convention

The Geneva Convention for the Improvement of the Condition of Wounded, Sick and Shipwrecked Members of Armed Forces at Sea. The Second Geneva Convention adapts the protections of the First Geneva Convention to reflect conditions at sea. It protects wounded and sick combatants while on board ship or at sea. Including

- Armed forces members who are wounded, sick or shipwrecked
- Hospital ships and medical personnel
- Civilians who accompany the armed forces

Specific provisions include:

Arts. 12, 18 This Convention mandates that parties in battle take all possible measures to search for, collect and care for the wounded, sick and shipwrecked.

Art. 22 Hospital ships cannot be used for any military purpose. They cannot be attacked or captured. The names and descriptions of hospital ships must be conveyed to all parties in the conflict.

Arts. 36-37 Religious, medical and hospital personnel serving on combat ships must be respected and protected. If captured, they are to be sent back to their side as soon as possible.

The Third Geneva Convention

The Geneva Convention Relative to the Treatment of Prisoners of War. The Third Geneva Convention sets out specific rules for the treatment of prisoners of war (POWs). The Convention's 143 articles require that POWs be treated humanely, adequately housed and receive sufficient food, clothing and medical care. Its provisions also establish guidelines on labour, discipline, recreation and criminal trial. Including

- Members of the armed forces
- Volunteer militia, including resistance movements
- Civilians accompanying the armed forces.

Specific provisions include:

Arts. 13-14, 16 Prisoners of war must not be subjected to torture or medical experimentation and must be protected against acts of violence, insults and public curiosity.

Arts. 25-27, 30 Captors must not engage in any reprisals or discriminate on the basis of race, nationality, religious beliefs, political opinions or other criteria.

Arts. 50, 54 POWs must be housed in clean, adequate shelter, and receive the food, clothing and medical care necessary to maintain good health. They must not be held in combat areas where they are exposed to fire, nor can they be used to "shield" areas from military operations.

Arts. 109, 110 Seriously ill POWs must be repatriated (returned home).

Art. 118 When the conflict ends, all POWs shall be released and, if they request, be sent home without delay.

The Fourth Geneva Convention

The Geneva Convention Relative to the Protection of Civilian Persons in Time of War. Civilians in areas of armed conflict and occupied territories are protected by articles of the Fourth Geneva Convention.

Specific provisions include:

Arts. 13, 32 Civilians are to be protected from murder, torture or brutality, and from discrimination on the basis of race, nationality, religion or political opinion.

Art. 18 Civilian hospitals and their staff are to be protected.

Arts. 33-34 Pillage, reprisals, indiscriminate destruction of property and the taking of hostages are prohibited.

Art. 40 Civilians cannot be forced to do military-related work for an occupying force.

Art. 54 They are to be paid fairly for any assigned work.

Art. 55 Occupying powers are to provide food and medical supplies as necessary to the population and maintain medical and public health facilities.

Arts. 55, 58 Medical supplies and objects used for religious worship are to be allowed passage.

Art. 132 Children, pregnant women, mothers with infants and young children, the wounded and sick and those who have been interned for a long time are to be released as soon as possible.

Religious viewpoint: Christian Realists

Not all Christians agree with the pacifist position on violence. A Christian Realist agrees that the teachings and life of Jesus does point us towards non-violence but they reject the idea that violence should never be allowed. They argue that in Matthew 21, Jesus uses force to end injustice in the Temple and that this points to a position whereby violence can be employed in some circumstances. Realists argue that individuals and states have different rights because they have different responsibilities. They argue that Jesus' moral teachings apply only to individuals and their interpersonal relations (private morality) and do not apply to states. Governing authorities are chosen by God (see Romans 13 v 1-7) to be responsible for the lives of others. The state therefore has the authority to act in ways that a private citizen may not (public morality). While pacifism must be the hallmark of a Christian's personal relationships, it cannot be extended wholescale into politics. This means that although it may be our individual responsibility to turn the other cheek, we also have a duty to act to protect others. One such realist was Dietrich Bonhoeffer, who although spent his life living by pacifist principles, joined a plot to kill Hitler during WW2. He stated of his actions that "it is better to do evil than to be evil."

Christian Realists Quotes

Matthew 21

12 Jesus entered the temple courts and drove out all who were buying and selling there. He overturned the tables of the money changers and the benches of those selling doves. 13 "It is written," he said to them, "'My house will be called a house of prayer,'[a] but you are making it 'a den of robbers.'[b]"

Romans 13

13 Let everyone be subject to the governing authorities, for there is no authority except that which God has established. The authorities that exist have been established by God. 2 Consequently, whoever rebels against the authority is rebelling against what God has instituted, and those who do so will bring judgment on themselves. 3 For rulers hold no terror for those who do right, but for those who do wrong. Do you want to be free from fear of the one in authority? Then do what is right and you will be commended. 4 For the one in authority is God's servant for your good. But if you do wrong, be afraid, for rulers do not bear the sword for no reason. They are God's servants, agents of wrath to bring punishment on the wrongdoer. 5 Therefore, it is necessary to submit to the authorities, not only because of possible punishment but also as a matter of conscience.6 This is also why you pay taxes, for the authorities are God's servants, who give their full time to governing. 7 Give to everyone what you owe them: If you owe taxes, pay taxes; if revenue, then revenue; if respect, then respect; if honour, then honour.

Matthew 5:9

"Blessed are the peacemakers, for they shall be called sons of God"

The Catechism of the Catholic Church

Legitimate defence can be not only a right but a grave duty for one who is responsible for the lives of others .The defence of the common good requires that an unjust aggressor be rendered unable to cause harm. For this reason, those who legitimately hold authority also have the right to use arms to repel aggressors against the civil community entrusted to their responsibility.

9 CONSEQUENCES OF WAR

Consequences of War - for humans

The consequences of war for humans are wide-ranging and can have devastating impacts on individuals, communities, and societies. Here are a few case studies that illustrate some of these consequences:

1. Syrian Civil War

The ongoing Syrian Civil War, which began in 2011, has resulted in immense human suffering. It has caused the death of hundreds of thousands of people, including civilians, and displaced millions within Syria and to neighbouring countries. The consequences include physical injuries, trauma, loss of homes and livelihoods, food insecurity, and limited access to healthcare and education. The war has also led to the recruitment of child soldiers, sexual violence, and the destruction of infrastructure and cultural heritage.

2. Rwandan Genocide

The Rwandan Genocide in 1994 resulted in the mass killing of an estimated 800,000 people over a span of 100 days. The consequences were widespread and included the loss of lives, displacement of millions, and long-lasting trauma for survivors. The genocide created a deep divide within society, leading to a breakdown of trust and social cohesion. Rebuilding the country has required significant efforts in reconciliation, justice, and addressing the psychological and social impacts of the genocide.

3. World War II

World War II, one of the deadliest conflicts in history, had numerous consequences for humans. The war led to the loss of millions of lives, including soldiers and civilians caught in the crossfire. It resulted in the displacement of millions through forced migrations and the destruction of cities and infrastructure. The Holocaust, a systematic genocide by Nazi Germany, resulted in the killing of six million Jews. The war also had long-lasting effects on the mental and physical health of survivors and shaped global politics and power dynamics for decades to come.

4. Afghanistan Conflict

The conflict in Afghanistan, ongoing since 2001, has had severe consequences for the Afghan population. It has resulted in significant civilian casualties, forced displacements, and widespread poverty. The war has also had detrimental effects on education and healthcare, limiting access to basic services for many Afghans. There have been reports of human rights abuses, including targeted killings, torture, and sexual violence. The consequences of the conflict have also spilled over into neighbouring countries, exacerbating regional instability.

Moral Issues

These case studies highlight the human toll of war, including loss of life, displacement, physical and psychological trauma, economic hardships, and the erosion of social fabric.

Consequences of War - for the environment

War can have severe consequences for the environment, ranging from immediate destruction caused by military operations to long-term environmental degradation. Here are a few case studies that illustrate the environmental consequences of war:

1. Gulf War (1990-1991): During the Gulf War, the Iraqi army set ablaze over 600 oil wells in Kuwait, resulting in one of the largest environmental disasters in history. The oil fires released large amounts of toxic pollutants into the air, causing air pollution and acid rain. The oil spillage also contaminated marine ecosystems in the Persian Gulf, affecting fish populations and damaging coral reefs.

2. Vietnam War (1955-1975): The extensive use of herbicides, particularly Agent Orange, by the United States military during the Vietnam War had long-lasting environmental effects. Agent Orange contained dioxin, a highly toxic chemical that contaminated soil and water, leading to deforestation, loss of biodiversity, and health issues for both humans and wildlife.

3. Balkan Wars (1991-2001): The Balkan Wars led to the deliberate targeting of industrial facilities, such as oil refineries and chemical plants. These attacks resulted in the release of hazardous substances into the environment, causing air, water, and soil pollution. The contamination affected agricultural lands, water sources, and public health, with long-term consequences for local communities.

4. Second Congo War (1998-2003): The conflict in the Democratic Republic of Congo resulted in widespread illegal mining, particularly for minerals like coltan, gold, and diamonds. This led to deforestation, habitat destruction, and soil erosion due to the unregulated extraction practices. The mining activities also fuelled armed conflict and contributed to human rights abuses.

Moral Issues

These case studies highlight the diverse ways in which war can impact the environment, including pollution, deforestation, habitat destruction, and loss of biodiversity. The consequences often extend beyond the immediate conflict, affecting the livelihoods and health of local communities for years to come.

Consequences of War - for the economy

War can have significant economic consequences, both in the short term and long term. Here are a few case studies that illustrate the economic impacts of war:

1. World War II (1939-1945): World War II had a profound impact on the global economy. It led to massive destruction of infrastructure, industries, and cities, resulting in significant economic losses. The war also caused disruptions in international trade and led to the displacement of millions of people, causing social and economic instability. However, the post-war period saw a surge in economic growth as nations invested in rebuilding their economies and industries.

2. Civil War in Sierra Leone (1991-2002): The civil war in Sierra Leone had severe economic consequences for the country. The conflict disrupted agricultural activities, which led to food shortages and increased dependence on imports. The war also resulted in the collapse of the mining industry, as rebel groups controlled the diamond mines and illegally traded the precious

stones. The economy of Sierra Leone suffered a significant decline during the war, and the country faced challenges in rebuilding its economy post-conflict.

3. Iraq War (2003-2011): The Iraq War had a substantial economic impact on Iraq. The conflict led to the destruction of infrastructure, including oil facilities, power plants, and transportation networks. The disruption in oil production and exports, which is a crucial source of revenue for Iraq, significantly impacted the country's economy. The war also resulted in a decline in foreign investment and increased government debt, leading to economic instability and challenges in rebuilding.

4. Yugoslav Wars (1991-2001): The series of conflicts in the former Yugoslavia had devastating economic effects. The wars led to the destruction of factories, infrastructure, and agricultural lands. Disruptions in trade and investment caused a decline in GDP and increased unemployment. The war also resulted in the displacement of millions of people, leading to social and economic disruptions.

Moral Issues

These case studies demonstrate the wide-ranging economic consequences of war, including destruction of infrastructure, decline in industries, disruptions in trade and investment, increased poverty and unemployment, and long-term economic instability. The recovery and rebuilding process post-conflict can be challenging and require significant investments and international assistance.

10 MODERN ARMAMENTS

Weapons of mass destruction

Weapons of mass destruction (WMD) are military weapons that have the capacity to cause significant harm and destruction on a large scale, targeting both human beings and infrastructure. They are characterized by their ability to inflict massive casualties, cause widespread damage, and have long-lasting effects. The term WMD was first used in 1937 by the Archbishop of Canterbury, Cosmo Gordon Lang. Lang said 'who can think without horror of what another widespread war would mean, waged as it would be with all the new weapons of mass destruction?' There are generally four categories of weapons that fall under the WMD classification:

1. Nuclear Weapons: Nuclear weapons derive their destructive power from nuclear reactions, specifically nuclear fission or fusion. These weapons release an enormous amount of energy in the form of an explosion, resulting in devastating effects such as blast waves, intense heat, and radiation. The detonation of a nuclear weapon can cause mass casualties and extensive damage over a wide area.

2. Chemical Weapons: Chemical weapons utilize toxic chemicals to harm, incapacitate, or kill people. They can be deployed through various means such as gas, liquids, or aerosols. Common chemical agents used in weapons include nerve agents (e.g., Sarin), blister

agents (e.g., Mustard gas), choking agents (e.g., Chlorine), and blood agents (e.g., Hydrogen cyanide). Chemical weapons can cause immediate harm upon contact with the human body and may have long-term health effects.

3. Biological Weapons: Biological weapons involve the use of living organisms or toxins derived from them to cause harm. These organisms or toxins can be bacteria, viruses, or other microorganisms that can cause diseases in humans, animals, or plants. Biological weapons can be deployed through the air, water, or through direct contact. They have the potential to spread rapidly and cause widespread illness, death, and disruption of essential services.

4. Radiological Weapons (Dirty Bombs): Radiological weapons, often referred to as dirty bombs, combine conventional explosives with radioactive material. Unlike nuclear weapons, these devices do not rely on nuclear reactions to cause destruction. Instead, their primary purpose is to spread radioactive material over a targeted area, contaminating the environment and causing fear, panic, and potential long-term health risks due to radiation exposure.

Chemical weapons expert Gert G Harigel argues that only nuclear weapons can truly be called WMD as they are completely 'indiscriminate'. Harigel calls chemical and biological weapons 'weapons of terror' when aimed against civilians and 'weapons of intimidation' when used against soldiers.

The former Secretary General of the United Nations, Kofi Annan, famously stated that small arms could be considered WMD because the fatalities they cause 'dwarf that of all other weapons systems – and in most years greatly exceed the toll of the atomic bombs that devastated Hiroshima and Nagasaki.

It is argued that the use of WMDs might only be justified in times of total war when targeting a country (including the civilian population) would be necessary in order to stop the support and supply of the war effort – i.e., by taking out the population, industry and natural resources.

Moral Issues with Weapons of Mass Destruction

The development, possession, and potential use of weapons of mass destruction give rise to several moral issues:

1. Humanitarian Concerns: The most prominent moral issue is the potential for mass casualties and the immense suffering inflicted on innocent civilians. WMD have the capacity to cause indiscriminate harm, leading to the loss of countless lives and severe injuries. The use of such weapons raises questions about the ethical implications of intentionally causing large-scale harm and whether the ends could ever justify such means.

2. Disproportionate Use of Force: WMD have the potential to cause disproportionate harm, far beyond what may be necessary for achieving military or strategic objectives. The use of these weapons can result in collateral damage to non-combatants, civilian infrastructure, and the environment. This raises concerns about the principle of proportionality in warfare and the ethical limits on the use of force.

3. Non-Proliferation and Arms Control: The development, possession, and potential use of WMD raise moral questions about the responsible stewardship of such weapons. The possession of these weapons by a state can create a power imbalance and increase the risk of their accidental or deliberate use. The moral imperative to prevent the proliferation of WMD and promote disarmament arises from the potential catastrophic consequences of their use.

4. Environmental and Long-Term Consequences: The use of WMD, particularly nuclear weapons, can have long-lasting and

irreversible environmental consequences. The radiation released can contaminate the air, soil, and water, affecting ecosystems and causing health problems for generations. The moral concern here lies in the potential harm inflicted on future generations and the responsibility to safeguard the environment for their well-being.

5. Moral Responsibility and Accountability: The final piece to the nuclear weapons puzzle is the idea of mutually assured destruction (MAD). Unlike other weapons of war, including biological and chemical weapons; nuclear weapons are often seen as being able to keep peace through their proliferation. This is down to the simple idea that after seeing the destructive capacity of these weapons, both trough war and nuclear testing. Nations will no longer engage in war with nuclear powers for fear of the use of these weapons. This is of course a two way street and times like the cold war of the 50's to the 80's have shown us how living in fear od "the bomb" has perhaps averted war.

This deterrent effect is not created through terrifying weapons like bio weapons, as nations often keep their developments secret to prevent their enemies developing antidotes. Due to the secretive nature of these weapons, nothing creates more fear than nuclear weapons.

Conventional weapons

A conventional war is a war between two or more states which is fought using conventional weapons and battlefield tactics. The two opposing forces can be well distinguished and the conventional weapons used primarily target the opposing army. A conventional war does not use chemical, biological or nuclear weapons (weapons of mass destruction).

Conventional weapons widely used in conflicts around the world. They include:

- Small arms and light weapons
- Sea and land mines
- (non-nuclear) bombs
- Shells
- Rockets
- Missiles
- Cluster munitions

Conventional weapons can acceptably be used in wars fought under the Geneva Convention. They are discriminate weapons and are managed and controlled by the combatants. This means that the results and consequences of their use are usually more predictable. The use of conventional weapons does not result in long term effects such as those felt by nuclear weapons. Certain types of conventional weapons are regulated or prohibited under the United Nations Convention on Certain Conventional Weapons.

The convention has five protocols:

- Protocol I restricts weapons with non-detectable fragments
- Protocol II restricts landmines, booby traps
- Protocol III restricts incendiary weapons
- Protocol IV restricts blinding laser weapons

- Protocol V sets out obligations and best practice for the clearance of explosive remnants of war.

There are 125 states who are party to this convention with some adopting all 5 protocols, but the minimum number required to be party to this convention is only 2 protocols.

Moral Issues with Conventional Weapons

The use of conventional weapons in warfare raises several moral issues such as:

1. Proportionality: One moral issue is ensuring that the use of conventional weapons is proportionate to the military objective and the threat faced. It is important to avoid disproportionate force that could result in unnecessary harm to civilians or damage to civilian infrastructure.

2. Non-combatant casualties: Conventional weapons, despite their more targeted nature compared to WMDs, can still cause significant harm to non-combatants, including civilians and humanitarian aid workers. The moral question arises on how to minimize civilian casualties and protect non-combatants from harm.

3. Indiscriminate impact: Some conventional weapons, such as cluster munitions or landmines, have indiscriminate effects and pose long-term risks to civilians even after conflicts end. The moral issue centres around the use of weapons that may continue to cause casualties and hinder post-conflict reconstruction efforts.

4. Arms trade and proliferation: The ethical concerns extend beyond the use of conventional weapons to their production, sale, and transfer. The global arms trade raises questions about the responsibility of states and corporations in supplying weapons to regions of conflict, potentially exacerbating violence and human suffering.

5. Humanitarian consequences: The use of conventional weapons can have severe humanitarian consequences, including displacement of populations, destruction of homes, schools, hospitals, and critical infrastructure. The moral issue revolves around the consideration of these consequences and the responsibility to protect civilian populations.

Smart weapons

Smart weapons, also known as precision-guided munitions or guided weapons, are a type of advanced military technology designed to precisely target and engage specific enemy targets while minimizing collateral damage and civilian casualties. These weapons employ various guidance systems, sensors, and technologies to improve accuracy, reduce errors, and increase effectiveness on the battlefield.

The term "smart" refers to the weapon's capability to autonomously or semi-autonomously navigate, track, and adjust its trajectory to hit a designated target with high precision. Unlike conventional weapons that rely solely on the skill of the operator and basic ballistic principles, smart weapons incorporate advanced guidance systems to actively steer towards their intended targets.

Inertial- Guided weapons- ones designed to cause damage with inertia but where explosions are unwanted e.g bombing fuel tanks.

Radio controlled weapons – ones which can be piloted after launch by an operator via radio.

Infrared guided missiles – ones which are controlled by computers to guide a bomb to a target using optical or heat sources which are identified by a human operator before launch.

Laser Guided weapons – ones which are often dropped from planes but are guided to the target by soldiers on the ground who use a laser to "paint" the desired target.

Radar Guided weapons – ones which will track and follow the radar signal which has been selected and locked before launch.

Satellite Guided weapons – ones which often use a GPS location to guide themselves to a target.

Smart weapons offer several potential advantages over conventional weapons. They can improve accuracy, reduce collateral damage, and minimize the risk to friendly forces. By hitting targets with precision, smart weapons can potentially reduce civilian casualties and infrastructure damage in conflict zones. However, it is important to note that even smart weapons are not foolproof, and the potential for unintended consequences or misuse still exists.

Moral Issues with Smart Weapons

The development and use of smart weapons have raised moral and ethical questions regarding their application and potential implications:

1. Target discrimination: While smart weapons are designed to improve target accuracy and minimize collateral damage, there is still the potential for mistakes or errors in target identification. The ability to distinguish between combatants and non-combatants, or between legitimate military targets and civilian infrastructure, remains a challenge. The risk of inadvertently targeting innocent civilians or causing disproportionate harm to civilian populations is a significant moral concern.

2. Accountability and responsibility: The use of smart weapons can sometimes distance operators from the immediate consequences of their actions. This raises questions of accountability and

responsibility. If a weapon is guided autonomously or through remote control, there may be a sense of detachment and reduced personal responsibility for the outcomes. This can lead to a potential moral hazard, where the decision to employ force becomes less transparent and the consequences less visible.

3. Human judgment and decision-making: Smart weapons rely heavily on algorithms, sensors, and technological systems to make decisions about target selection and engagement. This raises concerns about the role of human judgment in the use of force. There is a moral question of whether it is appropriate to delegate critical decisions to machines, especially when human lives are at stake.

4. Psychological and emotional consequences: The use of smart weapons can have psychological and emotional effects on operators and decision-makers. The ability to engage targets from a remote location, often thousands of miles away, may reduce the immediate psychological impact of warfare. However, it can also lead to moral distress and moral injury, where individuals grapple with the ethical implications of their actions and the consequences of their decisions.

11 THE ORIGINS OF THE UNIVERSE

Religious Views: Christianity

For the purposes of the Higher exam, we will take Christianity as our chosen 'religious view'. It is important to note from the outset that Christian views on the origins of the universe differ quite a lot – some will be very happy to reconcile scientific beliefs (e.g. the Big Bang) with their religious conviction, whereas others will reject scientific beliefs if they do not accord with their religious beliefs. The key thing that all Christians will have in common is that they believe that God is the ultimate creator of the universe.

This belief in God as creator of the universe stems from the very first words of the Bible: "In the beginning, God created the heavens and the earth" [Genesis 1:1].

The Genesis Account(s) of Creation

Depending on your view, the Bible has either one or two creation accounts in Genesis (the first book of the Bible). Some Christians view Genesis as one complete narrative, whereas others read it as two stories of the same creation event. If we are to split the stories in two, they are divided thus: **Genesis 1-2:3** and **Genesis 2:4-25**.

We can summarise the two accounts thus: the first is the 7 day creation account; the second is Eve being made out of Adam's rib.

It is important to be aware that, when talking about the origins of the universe, you should focus on the creation of the universe/world (rather than on the creation of life).

Genesis 1-2:3: The 7 Day Creation

1 In the beginning God created the heavens and the earth. **2** Now the earth was formless and empty, darkness was over the surface of the deep, and the Spirit of God was hovering over the waters. **3** And God said, "Let there be light," and there was light. **4** God saw that the light was good, and he separated the light from the darkness. **5** God called the light "day," and the darkness he called "night." And there was evening, and there was morning—the first day.

6 And God said, "Let there be a vault between the waters to separate water from water." **7** So God made the vault and separated the water under the vault from the water above it. And it was so. **8** God called the vault "sky." And there was evening, and there was morning—the second day.

9 And God said, "Let the water under the sky be gathered to one place, and let dry ground appear." And it was so. **10** God called the dry ground "land," and the gathered waters he called "seas." And God saw that it was good.

11 Then God said, "Let the land produce vegetation: seed-bearing plants and trees on the land that bear fruit with seed in it, according to their various kinds." And it was so. **12** The land produced vegetation: plants bearing seed according to their kinds and trees bearing fruit with seed in it according to their kinds. And God saw that it was good. **13** And there was evening, and there was morning—the third day.

14 And God said, "Let there be lights in the vault of the sky to separate the day from the night, and let them serve as signs to mark sacred times, and days and years, **15** and let them be lights in the vault of the sky to give light on the earth." And it was so. **16** God made two great lights—the greater light to govern the day and the lesser light to govern the night. He also made the stars. **17** God set them in the vault of the sky to give light on the earth, **18** to govern the day and the night, and to separate light from darkness. And God saw that it was good. **19** And there was evening, and there was morning—the fourth day.

20 And God said, "Let the water teem with living creatures, and let birds fly above the earth across the vault of the sky." **21** So God created the great creatures of the sea and every living thing with which the water teems and that moves about in it, according to their kinds, and every winged bird according to its kind. And God saw that it was good. **22** God blessed them and said, "Be fruitful and increase in number and fill the water in the seas, and let the birds increase on the earth." **23** And there was evening, and there was morning—the fifth day.

24 And God said, "Let the land produce living creatures according to their kinds: the livestock, the creatures that move along the ground, and the wild animals, each according to its kind." And it was so. **25** God made the wild animals according to their kinds, the livestock according to their kinds, and all the creatures that move along the ground according to their kinds. And God saw that it was good.

26 Then God said, "Let us make mankind in our image, in our likeness, so that they may rule over the fish in the sea and the birds in the sky, over the livestock and all the wild animals,[a] and over all the creatures that move along the ground."

27 So God created mankind in his own image,
    in the image of God he created them;
    male and female he created them.

28 God blessed them and said to them, "Be fruitful and increase in number; fill the earth and subdue it. Rule over the fish in the sea and the birds in the sky and over every living creature that moves on the ground."

29 Then God said, "I give you every seed-bearing plant on the face of the whole earth and every tree that has fruit with seed in it.

They will be yours for food. **30** And to all the beasts of the earth and all the birds in the sky and all the creatures that move along the ground—everything that has the breath of life in it—I give every green plant for food." And it was so.

31 God saw all that he had made, and it was very good. And there was evening, and there was morning—the sixth day.

2 Thus the heavens and the earth were completed in all their vast array.

2 By the seventh day God had finished the work he had been doing; so on the seventh day he rested from all his work. **3** Then God blessed the seventh day and made it holy, because on it he rested from all the work of creating that he had done.

The Key Points of the 7 Day Creation Account:

What are the key points of the Genesis 1-2:3 account? Perhaps the most important is that it asserts that God is the creator of everything, and that he creates *ex nihilo* (out of nothing).

God creates the heavens (i.e. the universe) and the earth, and he spends 6 days creating the earth and everything in it. God then rests on the 7th day.

What happens on each day?

1. **Day One**: light
2. **Day Two**: sky
3. **Day Three**: dry land, seas, trees, and plants
4. **Day Four**: the Sun, Moon, and stars
5. **Day Five**: birds (creatures that fly) and fish (creatures in the sea)
6. **Day Six**: land animals and, lastly, humans
7. **Day Seven**: rest

In the context of the origins of the universe (rather than the origins of life), only the first four days are strictly relevant.

Genesis 2:4-25: Eve out of Adam's Rib:

4 This is the account of the heavens and the earth when they were created, when the Lord God made the earth and the heavens.
5 Now no shrub had yet appeared on the earth[a] and no plant had yet sprung up, for the Lord God had not sent rain on the earth and there was no one to work the ground, **6** but streams[b] came up from the earth and watered the whole surface of the ground. **7** Then the Lord God formed a man[c] from the dust of the ground and breathed into his nostrils the breath of life, and the man became a living being.
8 Now the Lord God had planted a garden in the east, in Eden; and there he put the man he had formed. **9** The Lord God made all kinds of trees grow out of the ground—trees that were pleasing to the eye and good for food. In the middle of the garden were the tree of life and the tree of the knowledge of good and evil.
10 A river watering the garden flowed from Eden; from there it was separated into four headwaters. **11** The name of the first is the Pishon; it winds through the entire land of Havilah, where there is gold. **12** (The gold of that land is good; aromatic resin[d] and onyx are also there.) **13** The name of the second river is the Gihon; it winds through the entire land of Cush.[e] **14** The name of the third river is the Tigris; it runs along the east side of Ashur. And the fourth river is the Euphrates.
15 The Lord God took the man and put him in the Garden of Eden to work it and take care of it. **16** And the Lord God commanded the man, "You are free to eat from any tree in the garden; **17** but you must not eat from the tree of the knowledge of good and evil, for when you eat from it you will certainly die."
18 The Lord God said, "It is not good for the man to be alone. I will make a helper suitable for him."
19 Now the Lord God had formed out of the ground all the wild animals and all the birds in the sky. He brought them to the man to see what he would name them; and whatever the man called each living creature, that was its name. **20** So the man gave

names to all the livestock, the birds in the sky and all the wild animals.

But for Adam[f] no suitable helper was found. [21] So the Lord God caused the man to fall into a deep sleep; and while he was sleeping, he took one of the man's ribs[g] and then closed up the place with flesh. [22] Then the Lord God made a woman from the rib[h] he had taken out of the man, and he brought her to the man.

[23] The man said,

"This is now bone of my bones
    and flesh of my flesh;
she shall be called 'woman,'
    for she was taken out of man."

[24] That is why a man leaves his father and mother and is united to his wife, and they become one flesh.

[25] Adam and his wife were both naked, and they felt no shame.

The Key Points of the Second Genesis Creation Account

Unlike the first Genesis creation account, the order of creation is not divided into set days. Additionally, the order of creation is different. Here, God creates the earth and immediately makes man (Adam) "from the dust of the ground." God then places Adam into the Garden of Eden and creates wonderful trees and rivers and tells Adam that he is in charge of looking after the Garden of Eden. God realises that Adam will be lonely on his own, and so He creates all living creatures to keep Adam company. But none of these creatures are a suitable helper. So God puts Adam to sleep, takes one of his ribs, and from it, He creates woman (Eve).

There are some big differences to the first Genesis creation account: namely, humanity (specifically Adam) is created first here (whereas humans are created on the final day of creation in Genesis 1). Additionally, Adam and Eve are created separately here, whereas they appear together on Day 6 in the first account. Finally, all living creatures are created in between the creations of Adam and Eve (whereas all living creatures appear before humans in the first Genesis account).

Of course, the relevance of the second Genesis creation account for the origins of the universe is fairly limited – much of the story is about the creation of life. However, it does say that "God made the earth and the heavens." Therefore, many Christians will base their views on the origins of the universe on the first Genesis creation account.

How Should We Read The Genesis Creation Account(s)?

The different viewpoints that exist within Christianity about the origin of the universe can be explained by how each Christian chooses to interpret the Biblical creation account(s). In short, there are three ways that one can read Genesis:

1. Literally
2. Non-literally
3. As a myth/metaphor

A **literal** reading of Genesis means that we should take Genesis as historical and scientific fact – i.e. it happened exactly as described. Therefore, God did actually make everything in just 6 days, and he rested on the seventh. James Ussher (1581-1656) claimed that the first day of creation began at nightfall preceding Sunday, October 23rd, 4004 BC. Thus, the universe was created approximately 6,000 years ago.

A **non-literal** reading of Genesis means that we should understand that the writers of Genesis were inspired by God, and they wrote an interpretation of events so that the meaning is clear to people. The Genesis account teaches a religious truth (God created the universe) and was written in a way that people of the time, with limited scientific knowledge, would understand. Each 'day' in the Genesis account refers to the passage of time (i.e. millions of years).

Reading Genesis as a **myth/metaphor** recognises that there is a truth within the story, but that it is not scientific or historical truth. Instead, the story is designed to convey a religious truth (i.e. that God is the creator and loves his creation). Genesis is a story that has been handed down over generations to help people understand God's role in creation and our own existence. It is not intended to be taken as a scientific account of creation. This is similar to the moral truths that we can get from reading such mythical stories as King Arthur or Robin Hood.

Literal Religious Responses: Young Earth Creationism

If we are to read the first Genesis creation account literally, we probably fall into the camp of **Young Earth Creationism**. Young Earth Creationists (YECs) believe that the Bible is the direct word of God and, because God is perfect and infallible, it must therefore be totally true. If they say that any part of it is not factually true, then they are worried that non-Christians will say that none of the Bible is true (and, therefore, God doesn't exist). This means that YECs will disregard any scientific evidence that disagrees with the Genesis account.

YECs believe that the universe was created by God between 5,700 - 10,000 years ago. They believe that the scientific method demonstrates their belief in a supernatural creation. YECs believe in the literal word of the Bible, and as such Noah's Flood, the Fall of Man and the Tower of Babel (which all occur later in Genesis) are historic events. The universe/world was created in six, normal length days.

They also believe that early human lifespans were around 900 years, but dropped as a result of the inbreeding required, due to only 8 people surviving the flood (i.e. Noah and his family). The earth is not as old as scientists believe it to be. YECs disagree with the accuracy of carbon dating. The migration of the people from the collapse of the tower of Babylon caused the existence of native peoples such as Aborigines. While animals are all descended from those found on the ark, there is evolution occurring from that point.

YECs are often seen to be quite fundamental Christians.

Non-Literal Religious Responses: Old Earth Creationism(s)

A different Christian perspective is that of **Old Earth Creationism**, which takes a non-literal reading of the Genesis 1 account. Old Earth Creationists (OECs) essentially believe that the Earth may be older than Young Earth Creationism allows for, and thus the belief in Genesis may be more compatible with scientific findings. However, OECs still maintain that Genesis is the (non-literal) word of God and therefore contains historical and scientific truths.

Old Earth Creationism can be divided into two distinct ideas: Gap Creationism and Day-Age Creationism.

Gap Creationists believe that the six days in Genesis 1 are literal 24-hour days, but there is a significant gap of time between each one. Specifically, there is a gap of time between the two distinct creations in the first and second verses of Genesis (between the earth being created and then things appearing on it). This helps them adhere to scientific findings on the fossil record, age of the universe, age of the Earth, etc.

Day-Age Creationists believe that the six days in Genesis 1 are not literal 24 hour days. Instead, the days represent periods of time that can range from thousands to billions of years. This helps Day-Age Creationists accord their beliefs with scientific views on the age of the universe (13.8 billion years old), and the age of the Earth (4.5 billion years old). It also means that they can either incorporate the theory of evolution or reject it entirely. They use evidence such as the Cambrian Explosion (an event approximately 541 million years ago when all major animals started appearing in the fossil record) to support its views.

Myth/Metaphor Religious Responses:

Under this interpretation, Christians believe that the stories contained within the Bible did not necessarily happen as they are written (and they may not even have happened historically at all). However, the stories contain essential religious truths and are the best ways to express this. Therefore, the Genesis 1 account is a human-made story that tries to convey the truth about the origins of the universe – namely, that God is the creator of all things. The seven day creation metaphor works well because it is easy to understand and would have been an effective story-telling technique in the oral tradition (when stories used to be told, rather than written down). Fundamentally, this is not intended to be taken as a scientific account of creation.

St. Augustine was one such Christian thinker who believed that Genesis was not intended as a description of how God created the universe, but a story intended to reveal truths about the order in creation and the connection between God and humanity. Augustine said: "It must be said that our authors knew the truth about the nature of the skies, but it was not the intention of the Spirit of God, who spoke through them, to teach men anything that would not be of use to them for their salvation."

What Evidence Does Religion Use To Support These Explanations?

Creationism is often referred to by its adherents as '**Scientific Creationism**'. It is called this in order to convey a sense that there is scientific evidence to support the claims of creationism. It is quite obvious, however, that the claims of Scientific Creationism as often seen as 'pseudo-science' by other (non-Creationist) scientists.

So, what evidence do Creationists offer to support their views on the origins of the universe? Simply put, they offer the Bible as evidence. This is because they come from the position that the Bible is the word of God. Because God is all-knowing and perfect, this means that the words of the Bible are true. Therefore, if Genesis 1 says that the universe was created in six days, then – for Creationists – it *must* have been created in six days (as that's what God has said). As Creationist **Ken Ham** puts it: "No apparent, perceived, or claimed evidence in any field, including history and chronology, can be valid if it contradicts the Scriptural record."

The Creationist evidence outwith the Bible for the origins of the universe is slim. Instead, Young Earth Creationists would reject scientific theories (such as the Big Bang) and would try to find flaws in them (such as: how did the universe simply begin out of nothing?). Old Earth Creationists can be more compatible with scientific theories like the Big Bang, but – as noted earlier – they would reject any science that contradicts their Biblical story. So, OECs could potentially use some of the scientific evidence to support their beliefs – but only to a point!

Scientific Views On The Origins Of The Universe: The Big Bang

The main scientific belief about the origins of the universe is called the **Big Bang Theory** (BBT). In its simplest form, BBT states that all of the current and past matter in the universe came into existence at the same time – 13.8 billion years ago.

The idea was first talked about by a Belgian priest-scholar called **Georges Lemaître** in the 1920s. Although it wasn't taken very seriously until the 1960s, the Big Bang theory of the origins of the universe is now almost universally accepted.

Approximately 13.8 billion years ago, all matter was concentrated in a point of great density (a space-time **singularity**) which exploded. Out of that explosion came everything – all space, time, matter and energy. Immediately after the Big Bang the universe was thought to be smaller than the nucleus of an atom. A millisecond later the universe had expanded to the size of the sun. A few minutes after the Big Bang the first hydrogen and helium atoms were formed. Gradually these atoms then formed into gases which eventually would become the stars and all matter that we can see. Since the Big Bang, the universe has been expanding outwards and cooling.

What is the evidence for the Big Bang?

Evidence for BBT comes from a number of different scientific discoveries that build on each other. The first important principle is that of the **Doppler Effect** (first identified by Austrian physicist **Christian Doppler** in 1842). Doppler noted that there is a change in frequency of a moving object when observed by a stationary observer. For example, you may have noticed that when an ambulance or police car goes past, its siren is high-pitched as it comes towards you, and then becomes low-pitched as it goes away. This is because as the object approaches the observer the wavelength increases causing a rise in pitch, and the opposite occurs as the object passes and travels away from the observer.

Edwin Hubble (1889-1953) was an astronomer who noted that the Doppler Effect applied to stars that he observed in the universe. Hubble observed that as stars recede further into the distance they grow dimmer and redder. Hubble's brilliant observation was that the red shift of stars and galaxies was directly proportional to the distance of the star/galaxy from earth. That meant that things farther away from Earth were moving away faster. In other words, the universe must be expanding. This principle is known as **Red (Light) Shift**.

This supports the idea of a big bang: we can see that objects are moving further away, and therefore the universe is still expanding from a single starting point (i.e. the explosion of the Big Bang).

However, it wasn't until 1927 when **Georges Lemaître**, a Belgian physicist and Roman Catholic priest, independently proposed that the movement of the galaxies was due to the expansion of the universe. In 1931, he took this further by suggesting that the current expansion of the Universe meant that the father back in time one went, the smaller the Universe would be. At some point in the past, he argued, the entire mass of the universe would have been concentrated into a single point from which the very fabric of space and time originated.

BBT was given more substance when, in the 1960s, two young radio astronomers working for the Bell Telephone company, **Arno Penzias** and **Robert Wilson**, accidentally recorded an 'echo' of the Big Bang in the form of **cosmic microwave background radiation (CMBR)** which suggested that a huge explosion must have taken place at some point in the early history of the universe. CMBR fills all space and is the faint remnant glow of the Big Bang.

Subsequent discoveries by physicists such as **Stephen Hawking** (1942-2018) on black holes have added more weight to the evidence for the Big Bang.

Scientific Views On The Origins Of The Universe: Oscillating Universe Theory

Whilst BBT is *almost* universally accepted, there are other competing scientific beliefs about the origins of the universe. The main one is called **Oscillating Universe Theory** (OUT). In simple terms, OUT agrees that there was a Big Bang and that the universe is expanding. The theory states that the universe will keep on expanding until it becomes 'too heavy' and will start to fold in on itself. This is called the **Big Crunch**.

OUT theory, briefly considered (but ultimately rejected) by Albert Einstein in 1930, says that the universe follows an eternal series of oscillations: each beginning with a Big Bang and ending with a Big Crunch. The Big Crunch reduces the universe back down into a **singularity**, which then explodes in a new **Big Bang**. In the interim, the universe would expand for a period of time before the gravitational attraction of matter causes it to collapse back in on itself. In this way, this universe is just the latest incarnation of an infinite chain of universes.

What is the evidence for Oscillating Universe Theory?

Because OUT incorporates BBT, all the evidence used for BBT is applicable here. There is, as yet, no evidence for the Big Crunch, but it does make some sense according to mathematical models. Because we are unable to see beyond the beginning of our universe, the idea that there have been other universes that existed before this one is merely theoretical – there is no hard evidence to support this view. However, the reason why it is popular with some scientists is because it avoids the issues of trying to explain how the singularity came about. If there have always been universes in existence (i.e. the universe is, in effect, infinite) then we do not need to explain how the singularity originally occurred.

Scientific Views on The Origins of The Universe: Quantum Theory

The most notable issue with BBT is that it claims that the universe was nowhere and nothing but, somehow, there was an explosion that created everything. What exploded and where did it happen?

This issue arises as we are trying to understand the BBT through our own knowledge of Newtonian physics. In Newtonian physics all bodies obey fixed laws. There is an assumption that it is possible to predict their behaviour in every situation. Matter is considered to be solid and predictable, and all the laws of the universe could be discovered eventually. There is no need for reference to God, as science could provide all the answers. This certainty was lost with the development of **Quantum Theory**.

Quantum Theory is the set of physical laws that apply primarily on the very small scale, for entities the size of atoms or smaller. At the heart of quantum theory, lies the concept of uncertainty. Heisenberg's **uncertainty principle** demonstrated that the smallest component parts of matter are subject to unpredictable fluctuations. There appear to be spontaneous events – particles can appear from nothing.

Quantum Theory raises the following question: was the origin of the universe a quantum event? A quantum event is when something occurs that could not have happened according to the laws of classical (non-quantum) physics. So, could the origin of the universe be explained as a quantum event, but not be explicable through conventional (Newtonian) physics?

12 THE ORIGINS OF LIFE

Religious Views: Christianity

As we have seen, the Genesis accounts give a detailed account of both the origins of the universe and also the origins of life.
In the first creation account (Genesis 1-2:3), we see that all life on earth is created in a specific order. The key passage is **Genesis 1:20-27**:

[20] And God said, "Let the water teem with living creatures, and let birds fly above the earth across the vault of the sky." [21] So God created the great creatures of the sea and every living thing with which the water teems and that moves about in it, according to their kinds, and every winged bird according to its kind. And God saw that it was good. [22] God blessed them and said, "Be fruitful and increase in number and fill the water in the seas, and let the birds increase on the earth." [23] And there was evening, and there was morning—the fifth day.
[24] And God said, "Let the land produce living creatures according to their kinds: the livestock, the creatures that move along the ground, and the wild animals, each according to its kind." And it was so. [25] God made the wild animals according to their kinds, the livestock according to their kinds, and all the creatures that move along the ground according to their kinds. And God saw that it was good.
[26] Then God said, "Let us make mankind in our image, in our likeness, so that they may rule over the fish in the sea and the

birds in the sky, over the livestock and all the wild animals,[a] and over all the creatures that move along the ground."
27 So God created mankind in his own image,
 in the image of God he created them;
 male and female he created them.

Here we see the particular order of the origins of life over two days of creation: birds and fish are created on Day 5, and land animals and humans are created on Day 6.

The origins of life in the second Genesis account (**Genesis 2:4-25**) are somewhat different. As we have already said, there are some big differences to the first Genesis creation account: namely, humanity (specifically Adam) is created first here (whereas humans are created on the final day of creation in Genesis 1). Additionally, Adam and Eve are created separately here, whereas they appear together on Day 6 in the first account. Interestingly, Adam is made from dust – rather than out of nothing – which may suggest a dependency of humanity on the earth. Finally, all living creatures are created in between the creations of Adam and Eve (whereas all living creatures appear before humans in the first Genesis account).

What evidence does Religion use to support these beliefs?

As noted earlier, the evidence to support these beliefs rests upon the idea that the Bible is the word of God. If taken literally, this means that the Bible accounts of the origins of life are historically and scientifically true (because God is perfect and all-knowing and so the words of God must be true!).

A literal reading would be Young Earth Creationism (YEC). To recap: YECs believes that early human lifespans were around 900 years, but dropped as a result of the inbreeding required, due to only 8 people surviving the flood (i.e. Noah and his family). The earth is not as old as scientists believe it to be. YECs disagree with the accuracy of carbon dating. The migration of the people from the collapse of the tower of Babylon caused the existence of native peoples such as Aborigines. While animals are all descended from those found on the ark, there is evolution occurring from that point.

A non-literal reading would include Old Earth Creationism (OEC), specifically '**Progressive Creationism**'. This is the religious belief that God created new forms of life gradually over a period of hundreds of millions of years. As a form of Old Earth Creationism, it accepts mainstream geological and cosmological estimates for the age of the Earth.

In this view creation occurred in rapid bursts in which all 'kinds' of plants and animals appear in stages lasting millions of years. The Genesis account 'reveals' Creation in six days, but it was not performed in six days. The bursts are followed by periods of stasis or equilibrium to accommodate new arrivals. These bursts represent instances of God creating new types of organisms by divine intervention. It should be noted that these rapid bursts of life do not tally with the scientific view of evolution, but it does allow the Progressive Creationists to recognise that the fossil record dates different forms of life occurring over millions of years.

Obviously, a mythical/metaphorical reading would see these Biblical stories of the origins of life as exactly that – stories. On this understanding, the important theme is that God has creative power and that humanity is a special part of God's creation (thus, only humanity can form a true relationship with God and gain access to heaven, etc).

Scientific views on the Origins of Life: Evolution

Any question that asks about scientific views on creation or about the creation of life, will need to refer to **Charles Darwin's** Theory of **Evolution**.

Darwin was not the first to pose a theory that all life was related and that animals were somehow naturally adapted to their environment, but he is very much the godfather of this theory as he produced the most complete scientific picture of the origins of life.

Before Darwin, there was a recognition that many animals were well suited to their environment; birds have wings, fish have gills etc, but this was often credited to some kind of designer who oversaw this process.

In 1852 Herbert Spencer an English philosopher coined the phrase **"survival of the fittest"** but is was Darwin's 1859 work *"On the Origin of Species by Means of Natural Selection, or the Preservation of Favoured Races in the Struggle for Life"* (which is a catchy title! You can just call it *On the Origin of Species*) where he posed a theory of how complex organisms, evolved to improve their chances of survival in a particular environment and expressed much of the evidence that he had found to back up this theory.

Charles Darwin's theory of evolution had three main components:

> 1. that variation occurred randomly among members of a species
> 2. that an individual's traits could be inherited by its offspring
> 3. the struggle for existence would allow only those with favourable traits to survive

Darwin studied variation in plants, animals and fossils during a five-year voyage around the world in the 19th century. He visited four continents on the ship HMS Beagle, including a five week visit to the Galapagos Islands (near Ecuador) where he studied finches.

By studying the finches, Darwin saw that there was a remarkable diversity in beak form and function. For example, some had beaks that were good for breaking open nuts, whilst others had beaks that were better for eating fish. Darwin concluded that, because of a notable lack of other birds on the island, these finches had 'adapted' to their environment over many generations – thus explaining the differences between them.

This led Darwin to conclude that species change and mutate over time. These mutations are random and can be beneficial or a hindrance (or no effect at all!). If they are beneficial, they will help that organism be better suited to their natural environment. This will allow that organism to survive for longer and reproduce, thus passing on the advantageous mutation to its offspring. Those without these beneficial mutations ('adaptations') will die out. Thus, over time, the organism with the beneficial adaptation becomes the dominant form of that species.

In sum:

- There is variation within species caused by mutation (i.e. some penguins are taller than others)
- All living things tend to multiply beyond the available food supply
- There is a struggle for survival
- Some variations give an advantage to the individuals that exhibit them (and vice versa)
- These individuals are more likely to survive in the struggle for life

- Those individuals live long enough to produce offspring
- The offspring will inherit the parent's advantageous trait
- Over generations, the advantageous trait becomes more common

What Is The Evidence for Evolution?

1: The Fossil Record

Fossils are the preserved remains of previously living organisms, dating from the distant past (including from many millions of years ago). It is important to note that the fossil record is not complete or unbroken: most organisms never fossilize, and even the organisms that do fossilize are rarely found by humans. Nevertheless, the fossils that humans have collected offer unique insights into evolution over long timescales.

Fossil remains have been found in rocks of all ages. Fossils of the simplest organisms are found in the oldest rocks, and fossils of more complex organisms in the newest rocks. This supports Darwin's theory of evolution, which states that simple life forms gradually evolved into more complex ones.

Fossils document the existence of now-extinct species, showing that different organisms have lived on Earth during different periods of the planet's history. They can also help scientists reconstruct the evolutionary histories of present-day species. For instance, some of the best-studied fossils are of the horse lineage.

Using these fossils, scientists have been able to reconstruct a large, branching 'family tree' for horses and their now-extinct relatives. Changes in the lineage leading to modern-day horses, such as the reduction of toed feet to hooves, may reflect adaptation to changes in the environment.

There are gaps in the fossil record because many early forms of life were soft-bodied, which means that they have left few traces behind. What traces there were may have been destroyed by geological activity. This is why scientists cannot be certain about how life began.

2: Speciation

Speciation is the formation of new and distinct species in the course of evolution.

Darwin thought of evolution as "descent with modification": a process in which species change and give rise to new species over many generations. He proposed that the evolutionary history of life forms a branching tree with many levels, in which all species can be traced back to an ancient common ancestor.

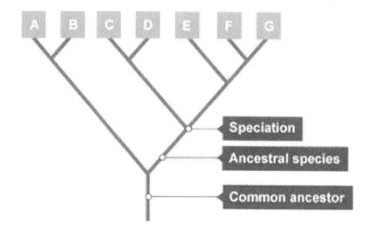

In this evolutionary tree, species A and B share a recent common ancestor. Species A is therefore most similar to species B. Species F and G also share a recent, yet different, common ancestor, which itself shared a common ancestor with species E. All seven species share a common ancestor, probably from the distant past.

If two or more species share a unique physical feature, such as a complex bone structure or a body plan, they may all have inherited this feature from a common ancestor. Physical features shared due to evolutionary history (a common ancestor) are said to be **homologous**.

The image below shows what could happen to an animal population, which is separated into two isolated groups by a geographical feature, such as a mountain or river.

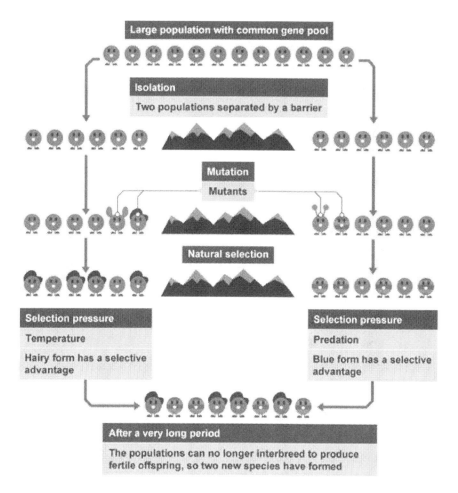

Charles Darwin described the speciation of finches after his studies of the birds on the Galapagos Islands, which are a group of islands roughly 1,000 km off the coast of Ecuador. Darwin noticed that the finches on the different islands were similar to each other.

However, Darwin's studies revealed that the finches had wide variations in their size, beaks and claws from island to island. The finches' beaks differed depending on the local food source. Darwin concluded that because the islands were distant from the mainland, the finches that had arrived there had changed over time.

3: Variations within a species

Even within the same species, variations exist that can point to the truth of evolution. A famous example is the peppered moth. The evolution of the peppered moth is an evolutionary instance of directional colour change in the moth population as a consequence of air pollution during the Industrial Revolution. In short, there are two colours of peppered moth – light and dark. Prior to 1820, the darker-coloured peppered moth was quite rare. However, the darker coloured peppered moth population became the dominant colour as the pollution caused by the Industrial Revolution increased. As surfaces became covered with soot, the lighter-coloured peppered moth became an easy target for predators, whereas the darker-coloured peppered moth blended into the (change of) environment well.

In a short space of time, most peppered moths were of the darker colour. By the end of the 19th century it almost completely outnumbered the original light-coloured type. As pollution decreased after the Industrial Revolution, and surfaces became cleaner again, the darker-coloured peppered moth was now an easy target for predators. Thus, the lighter-coloured peppered moth became the dominant colouring of the species again.

In 1978, Sewall Wright described it as "the clearest case in which a conspicuous evolutionary process has actually been observed." This example shows that, even within a species, certain mutations – in this case, colouring – can have evolutionary advantages and therefore allow the organisms with that characteristic to flourish.

4: Vestigial Organs

Vestigial organs (or 'vestigial structures') are organs that have lost their use through evolution. In humans, examples of vestigial structures include the appendix and the coccyx.

The coccyx, or tailbone, is the remnant of a lost tail. All mammals have a tail at some point in their development; in humans, it is present for a period of 4 weeks, and is most prominent in human embryos 31–35 days old. The tailbone, located at the end of the spine, has lost its original function in assisting balance and mobility, though it still serves some secondary functions, such as being an attachment point for muscles, which explains why it has not degraded further.

This is evidence for evolution because it shows that human ancestors had a tailbone but, because of a change in environment or a mutation of other body parts, the tailbone was no longer necessary and so has become redundant.

5: Similarities in Developing Embryos

Following on from the tailbone example, we also see that some homologous structures can only be seen in embryos. For example, all vertebrate embryos (including humans) have gill slits during early development. The developmental patterns of these species become different later on. Human gill slits develop into the jaw and inner ear. Homologous embryonic structures show that the developmental programs of vertebrates are variations on a similar plan that existed in their last common ancestor.

6: DNA

At the most basic level, all living organisms share the same genetic material (DNA). This suggests that all living organisms descended from a common ancestor, and that this common ancestor had DNA as its genetic material.

Going further, we see that all living organisms share the same, or highly similar, genetic codes. This also points towards a shared common ancestor. Different species share the same gene. For example: humans, cows, chickens, and chimpanzees all have a gene that encodes the hormone insulin, because this gene was already present in their last common ancestor. The more DNA differences in these genes, the more distantly the species are related. Using the example of insulin: human and chimpanzee insulin proteins are much more similar (about 98% identical) than human and chicken insulin proteins (about 64% identical), showing that humans and chimpanzees are more closely related than humans and chickens.

13 RELIGION AND SCIENCE

Can Religious and Scientific Views on Origins Be Compatible?

This is the heart of your Evaluation! It is up to you to decide whether the religious and scientific viewpoints outlined here can be compatible with each other. However, here are some pointers that may help you…

The Creationist Stance

As you know, Creationists can incorporate some scientific ideas – but only as long as they align with their Biblically-based beliefs (i.e. as long as the science fits in with the Genesis account).

One of the most notable Creationists is the Australian evangelist Ken Ham. He said: "No apparent, perceived, or claimed evidence in any field, including history and chronology, can be valid if it contradicts the Scriptural record."

Ken Ham also founded the Creationist website *Answers in Genesis* (https://answersingenesis.org/), which is a useful resource for seeing how Creationists view scientific findings, and how they respond to the scientific evidence that contradicts Genesis. Be sure to use your critical thinking skills when reading some of the answers on there!

The Religious (non-Creationist) Stance

It is fair to say that (Young/Old Earth) Creationists are quite fundamental Christians. It is important to understand that the vast majority of Christians throughout the world are <u>not</u> Creationists. However, they do believe in God and in God's creative power. It is likely that many Christians will understand the Genesis accounts in a mythical/metaphorical way and be open to the scientific evidence, seeing it as evidence of God's wonderful creative power and imagination.

The Fundamental (Atheistic) Scientific Stance

A number of scientists are quite vocal in their opposition to religion – **Richard Dawkins** being one of the most outspoken. For Dawkins, science can (or, at least, one day will) explain everything without the need to invoke a supreme deity (i.e. God). Dawkins is what one might term a 'militant atheist' – he has an extreme opposition to religion and does not believe in God, and therefore he is unlikely to think that there is any compatibility between religious and scientific beliefs about the origins of the universe/life. As Dawkins himself says: "I am against religion because it teaches us to be satisfied with not understanding the world."

The Religious-Scientific Stance

A number of scientists are also religious, and therefore believe that scientific beliefs and can be compatible with religious beliefs. **John Polkinghorne** was one such religious scientist, and believed that God was the ultimate answer to the question 'why is there something rather than nothing?'.

As Polkinghorne said, "As a Christian believer I am, of course, a creationist in the proper sense of the term, for I believe that the mind and the purpose of a divine Creator lie behind the fruitful history and remarkable order of the universe which science explores. But I am certainly not a creationist in that curious North American sense, which implies interpreting Genesis 1 in a flat-footed literal way and supposing that evolution is wrong."

On debating questions of origins with Dawkins, Polkinghorne said: "debating with Dawkins is hopeless, because there's no give and take. He doesn't give you an inch. He just says no when you say yes."

Non-Overlapping Magisteria (NOMA)

Continuing from the idea that the creation stories are written to explore a deeper truth about the universe and existence (i.e. that they should be read as a myth/metaphor), 20th Century Christian philosopher **Stephen Jay Gould** has described the position he calls Non-Overlapping Magisteria (NOMA).

This proposes that science and religion each represent different areas of inquiry – Fact vs Values. This suggests that there are limits to each of their teaching authority ('magisterium') and the two do not overlap. This would suggest that there is no conflict between scientific theories and religious teachings as there is in fact no overlap of content and therefore no conflict.

As Gould says, "Science tries to document the factual character of the natural world, and to develop theories that coordinate and explain these facts. Religion, on the other hand, operates in the equally important, but utterly different, realm of human purposes, meanings, and values—subjects that the factual domain of science might illuminate, but can never resolve."

Agent and Mechanism Theory

A further manner in which religion and science could be seen as compatible is by not rejecting scientific explanations such as big bang but rather seeing these explanations as the mechanism that God has used for his creation. If the Genesis stories simply point to the idea that God is the creator, Christians can then see God as the creator of Big Bang and the designer of Evolution.

Big Bang as Mechanism

In the eyes of many Christians the greatest problem with BBT is not in the question of 'if and when' the big bang happened, but of 'how and why'. Questions on where or how the quarks responsible for causing the big bang did so remain unanswered. This is not to say that there are not answers to this question, but for many it is more reasonable to believe that God is the 'agent' who caused the big bang. This solution also addresses the issue of why the universe exists: as the famous physicist **Stephen Hawking** noted, "Why does the universe bother to exist?" The belief that God created the universe for human existence addresses this issue as well.

Evolution as Mechanism

The theory of Evolution (TOE) is more complete than BBT, and given that the evidence is here on planet earth for us to explore it is a far easier question to address. However, some Christians feel that it is still possible to believe that evolution is in fact God's mechanism for creation. British theologian **F R Tennant** noted that: "The survival of the fittest presupposes the arrival of the fit, and throws no light thereupon."

The belief that God creates the first life forms and then allows for evolution to run a course that he is fully aware will result in the creation of humanity is still within the scope of the TOE. God also addresses another major issue with TOE: that human beings possess characteristics which have no survival benefit.

F R Tennant notes man's "moral capacity" and our "aesthetic awareness." Human beings spend a lot of time enjoying beautiful scenery, or appreciating music and art and yet this has no survival advantage. He argued that man's aesthetic awareness suggests the 'invisible and mysterious presence of God' in the process of man's evolution.

The Anthropic Principle

Many Christians have used scientific advances as evidence to support their belief. The **Anthropic Principle** suggests that the Big Bang could so easily have unfolded in a way that prevented life from forming. If any of the major constants of the universe (i.e. the charge of the electron, the force of gravity, the earth's distance from the sun, etc) were different, we would not have been here and life would not have evolved. However, the fact that the universe did provide the conditions needed for the formation of life suggests that the laws of the universe were very carefully set for this purpose.

The Anthropic Principle therefore claims that the universe is constructed for the development of intelligent life. The universe is *anthropo* (mankind) *centric* (centred on). The Anthropic Principle therefore denies that the universe and life came about by chance. This argument hinges on the improbability that the universe can support life.

John Barrow and Frank Tipler wrote about the Anthropic Principle, summing it up thus: "Imagine a universe in which one or another of the fundamental constants of physics is altered by a few percent one way or the other. Man could never come into being in such a universe. That is the central claim of the Anthropic Principle."

Probability of the BBT

Renowned French mathematician, Emile Borel, discussed in depth the law of probability known as the Single Law of Chance: a law that he said "events whose probability is extremely small never occur". In his discussion on the probabilities of certain cosmic events, he argues from mathematical calculations that the probability of the big bang occurring in the Universe is less than one in $10^{340,000,000}$ (i.e. a one with 45 zeros after it), human beings intuitively categorize that event as so unlikely that we consider it to be an impossible event.

Probability of Evolution Forming Life

Evolutionist Harold Morowitz estimated the probability of the formation of the smallest and simplest living organism to be one in $10^{340,000,000}$ He further stated: imagine 10^{54} blind persons each with a scrambled Rubik's cube, and try to conceive of the chance of them all simultaneously arriving at the solved form. You then have the chance of arriving by random shuffling at just one of the many biopolymers on which life depends.

Ockham's Razor

Ockham's Razor is a principle devised by **William of Ockham** according to which, other things being equal, explanations that posit fewer entities, or fewer kinds of entities, are to be preferred to explanations that posit more. In basic terms, it means that the simplest solution tends to be the right one.

Given the improbability of the creation of a person-friendly universe, many Christians and scientists may apply the principle of Ockham's razor. However, the conclusion they come to will depend on whether they think that God is a more simple answer than an entirely natural explanation (like the one proposed by Dawkins and others). Dawkins would say that God is not a simple answer as it leads to further questions such as 'why does God exist?'. Christians may say that God is a simple answer as it avoids having to explain how we beat extremely long odds and exist in a universe which is able to support life.

Printed in Great Britain
by Amazon

27183053R00074